THE
Marvelous
MICROWAVE

D1737957

BY JANE TRITTIPO

Copyright © 1996 Jane Trittipo
Library of Congress Catalog Card Number: 96-85881
ISBN 0-9621242-1-4

Cover and Book Design: David Freedman, Karen Trittipo
Published by: Creative Cookery
             PO Box 437
             Alamo, CA 94507-2312

First Edition
First printing October 1996

This book is dedicated
To our daughters and their husbands
Karen and David
Lynn and Diego
whose artistic support and
ongoing input
have kept me young at heart
and eager to share
what I know about
the marvels of
microwave cooking.

CONTENTS

INTRODUCTION

If someone offered you a marvelous appliance that would change your life by helping you prepare healthy, low fat, good-tasting meals in one fourth the time, you'd buy it, wouldn't you?

You probably already have that marvelous appliance. It's your microwave oven! You may have used it for reheating coffee or leftovers. But your microwave can do so much more for you. It's a fabulous, time saving, energy saving, healthy way to prepare food. This book will show you how to use it more effectively as you learn to microcook with the recipes I've included.

To make your learning journey easier, follow these three rules:

1 Every day, microcook one food.

2 Don't turn on your cook top burner. Use your microwave instead. Whenever you find yourself reaching for a pot or pan to use on the cook top put it back and find a microsafe container. Most foods can be cooked faster in the microwave and usually with fewer dishes to wash! Remember – any food cooked on the stovetop can be microcooked.

3 Plan your weekly menus using recipes from this book. Purchase the ingredients, follow the step-by-step recipes and be prepared for surprises.

Healthy eating is the norm these days. Most of the recipes feature low or nonfat cooking which is what healthy eating is all about. Unlike sautéing, microwave cooking is oil free. The microwave allows you to cook healthy food while preserving nutrients without sacrificing flavor or spending hours over a hot cook top.

The microwave cooks vegetables, seafood and poultry without the need of water, oils or fats. Because microwave cooking retains moisture vegetables retain their nutrients and bright colors. Seafood and poultry are succulent and full of flavor.

It is the vibration of molecules as the microwaves pass through the food that actually creates the heat that cooks the food in the microwave. High Power actually means the magnetron tube is producing power at the fullest wattage of your microwave. If you microcook on Medium Power, (50%) – it simply means the microwave is ON half the time and OFF half the time, therefore producing a gentler cooking condition.

I have included complete concise one or two page easy-to-follow recipes. Each chapter begins with a listing of recipes and a brief discussion of ways to use your microwave for that type of food. To encourage your pursuit in this new world of microwave cooking, personal comments and presentation suggestions accompany every recipe. I have also given suggestions for adapting your family's favorite recipes to microwave cooking. In our fast paced lives we tend to eat boring meals or junk food. You can change all this. I have included enough 'plate-fixed dinners' (listed in the index) to help you serve good food fast. These recipes use fresh ingredients, microcooked together and served on a dinner plate!

Because of my inquisitive nature and chemistry background, I delight in researching and experimenting with new ways to use the microwave. This experimenting led to writing my popular microwave cookbook *The Everyday Gourmet* (1988). Since that first book, I have enjoyed teaching others the joys of microwave cooking via radio and TV, and through presentations for various organizations' fund raising efforts. It is my pleasure to share my microwave knowledge with you via the pages of this book. I urge you to use your *Marvelous Microwave* every single day.

Jane Trittipo,
Alamo, California

ACKNOWLEDGMENTS

Writing a cookbook is a very exciting adventure. As with anything else in life I could not do it alone. I needed the support of family, friends and experts as I journeyed through the maze of desktop publishing. I gratefully accepted the artistic expertise and advice of David Freedman, my son-in-law and our daughter Karen Trittipo, graphic designers in New York City. They designed the book cover and general layout. My friend Linda Johnson in Weston, Connecticut joyously accepted my plea to format the book. Thank you, Linda, for sharing your expertise via fax and modem. A special thanks to my good friend Bill Dent for taking the back cover picture and to my friends, Jo Harberson, and Nita and Johnson Mossman for their endless hours of proofing and editing. My printer Wesley Turner's advice, support and problem-free production was especially helpful. I also had unending encouragement and recipe advice from my many friends at St. Timothy's Episcopal Church, Danville and from my P.E.O. and AAUW friends as well.

My family helped me understand how young families work, eat and live in these exciting hectic times. Thank you Karen, David, Lynn and Diego. To Casey and Aaron my grandchildren, thanks for liking my cookies and licking my spoons. A most special thanks to my supportive husband, Tom. His fabulous sense of humor and reassuring calmness helped me over many obstacles, including piles of dirty dishes. Thanks for being by my side.

To all who helped me see this book become a reality, my heartfelt thanks.

APPETIZERS

Bacon Wrappped Almond Stuffed Dates

Cheese Topped Potato Bites

Nacho Potato Rounds

Quesadilla Appetizers

Jalapeño Pepper Jelly

Mexican Mushrooms

Quick and Easy Southwest Appetizer

Pepper Pizza

Pita Pizza

Mushrooms à la Grecque

Tortilla Pinwheels

Pesto Sauced Tortellini–Broccoli Skewers

Polenta Triangles

Pork Medallions with Three Dipping Sauces

Sesame Pea Dip

Crusty Goat Cheese Rounds

Spinach Wrapped Chicken Bites with Curry Dipping Sauce

Sticky Wings

Spinach and Scallop Terrine with Caper Sauce

A PARTY OFFERING only appetizers with various beverages and a finale of desserts and coffee is a popular way to entertain. Guests love to graze and the microwave is a marvelous appliance when it comes to making appetizers. Whether it be popcorn or an elegant seafood terrine, your microwave will make preparation a breeze.

If you are microcooking several appetizer pieces, be certain to arrange them in a circle around the outer edge of a microsafe plate before cooking them. If you place any in the center of the plate they will not cook very quickly. Pastry type foods and deep fried appetizers are best prepared the conventional way.

Many appetizers will freeze well. If you store them in zippered bags you can take out a few at a time. Remember to label the bags, as things sometimes look a little different when frozen.

If you have a favorite appetizer recipe and you want to cook it in the microwave, combine the ingredients, decreasing the liquid slightly. To test, place a small portion in the microwave on a microsafe plate and micro-cook on High Power in 30 second intervals. Experiment: it's fun and usually quite successful.

BACON WRAPPED ALMOND STUFFED DATES

8 slices bacon
16 pitted dates
16 almonds

1 Cut bacon slices in half. Place slices on bacon rack or a paper towel lined microsafe plate. Microcook on High Power 3-5 minutes or just until slightly cooked but not crisp.

2 Stuff an almond in each date, wrap a piece of bacon around each almond stuffed date and secure with a toothpick.

3 Arrange 8 wrapped dates in a circle on a bacon rack or microsafe plate, cover loosely with waxed paper and microcook on High Power 2 minutes, turn over and microcook 2 additional minutes until they are crisp and brown. Repeat with remaining 8 wrapped dates.

4 Remove to a serving platter and serve hot.

• Makes 16 pieces

The first time I prepared these stuffed dates they were a disaster! The high concentration of fat and sugar caused them to cook more quickly than I had anticipated. Be forewarned; follow the directions and don't overcook!

Talk about easy!
And they're healthy
and hearty as well.
Your friends will really
like these tasty bites.

CHEESE TOPPED POTATO BITES

2 medium potatoes, about 1 pound
2 ounces low fat shredded cheese (Mozzarella, etc.)
1/4 teaspoon garlic powder
1/4 teaspoon chili powder
1/4 teaspoon dried basil
& dash of pepper

1. Scrub potatoes and prick each with a fork. Wrap each potato in a paper towel and place in microwave oven. Microcook on High Power 4-5 minutes. Turn potatoes over and microcook on High Power another 4-5 minutes. Unwrap, let cool and refrigerate.

2. When chilled, cut into 1/4-inch slices and top with sprinkling of cheese.

3. Combine the garlic powder, chili powder, dried basil, and pepper in a small bowl. Sprinkle the herb mixture evenly over the cheese topped potato slices.

4. Arrange 8 potato slices around the outer rim of a paper towel lined microsafe plate. Microcook on High Power 30-40 seconds, or just until cheese melts. Repeat with remaining slices.

• Makes approximately 16 slices.

NACHO POTATO ROUNDS

1 large potato, washed; do not peel
2 tablespoons taco sauce
3/4 cup shredded Cheddar Cheese
1 (4-ounce) can chopped green chiles

1 Slice the potato into 1/4-inch rounds, using a knife or the slicing blade of your processor.

2 Place 10 potato rounds in a circle on a round microsafe plate. Brush lightly with taco sauce. Cover with plastic wrap and microcook on High Power 5 minutes or until the potatoes are just fork tender.

3 Sprinkle with cheese and chiles. Microcook on High Power 2 minutes or until the cheese is completely melted. Allow to cool a few minutes before serving. Repeat with any remaining slices.

• Makes 8-12 slices

Potato rounds make a wonderful base for bite-sized appetizers. When your dinner features Mexican food, offer these simple appetizers. Talk about easy! And they're healthy and hearty as well. Your friends will really like these tasty bites. These quesadilla wedges are always a hit at parties.

They are quickly assembled and only require a few minutes in the microwave— just long enough to melt the cheese.

QUESADILLA APPETIZERS

    6 ounces grated Cheddar cheese
1/2 cup chopped fresh cilantro
    2 green onions, sliced
    1 (5.8-ounce) can whole kernel corn, drained
    1 (4-ounce) can chopped green chiles
    8 (6-inch) flour or corn tortillas
      salad greens for garnish
      taco sauce
  & sour cream

1   In a medium size bowl, mix cheese, chopped cilantro, green onions, corn and chopped green chiles. Spoon an equal amount of mixture onto 4 tortillas. Cover each tortilla with one of the 4 remaining tortillas to make 4 quesadillas.

2   Place 1 quesadilla on a microsafe plate. Microcook on High Power 1 minute 30 seconds, turning quesadilla over after 1 minute. Let cool 2 minutes before cutting.

3   Cut each quesadilla into 6 wedges. Arrange wedges on a large serving plate or individual plates. Garnish with salad greens and serve with taco sauce and sour cream.

•   Makes 48 wedges

JALAPEÑO PEPPER JELLY

    5 medium canned jalapeño peppers, seeded
    1 medium green pepper, seeded
  2/3 cup distilled white vinegar
  2/3 cup cider vinegar
5 1/2 cups sugar
  1/4 teaspoon crushed dried red peppers
  1-2 dashes red pepper sauce
    2 (3-ounce) packets liquid fruit pectin

1 In a processor (steel knife) or a blender, process the jalapeño and green peppers until finely chopped.

2 Pour the pepper mixture into a large microsafe bowl. Add the distilled vinegar, cider vinegar, sugar, dried red peppers and red pepper sauce. Microcook on High Power about 8 minutes or until mixture boils. Continue to boil mixture 3 minutes. Stir in pectin.

3 Microcook on High Power 1 minute or until mixture boils.

4 Skim off foam; pour into sterilized jars. Cool to room temperature. Cover and refrigerate up to 3 months.

• Makes 4-5 cups

It is nice to have this flavorful appetizer spread ready to serve during the holiday season when guests drop in. Place a festive bowl of this jelly, a small bowl of softened cream cheese and a few crackers or slices of French bread on a festive tray. Instantly you have an elegant, appetizing presentation. Jars of this jelly make a lovely hostess gift any time of year—include the recipe too!

Stuffed mushrooms are always a hit at any party. This recipe is very fast and easy to prepare and it's tasty and colorful as well. I have also used this as an entrée for two, using two large (4-6 inch) mushrooms with the same stuffing. Add a green salad and a glass of cerveza and dinner is ready in no time.

MEXICAN MUSHROOMS

12 fresh (1-2 inch) mushrooms,
   cleaned and stemmed
   (about 1/2 pound)
1/4 pound ground beef
 1 tablespoon taco sauce
 1 small tomato, chopped
1/2 cup grated sharp Cheddar cheese

1 Place ground beef in a small microsafe bowl. Microcook on High Power 2 minutes, stirring after 1 minute. Drain any liquid.

2 Combine the ground beef and taco sauce. Fill prepared mushroom caps.

3 Sprinkle chopped tomato on filling and top with grated cheese.

4 Place 12 mushrooms in a circle on a microsafe plate and microcook on High Power 1-2 minutes or until cheese melts.

• Serves 4 as an appetizer, 2 as an entrée

QUICK AND EASY SOUTHWEST APPETIZER

While this appetizer is not exactly healthy eating, it certainly is fast and the presentation always impresses guests.

  1 (16-ounce) can refried beans
  1 small onion, chopped
1/2 (7-ounce) bottle medium hot, red taco sauce
  1 (2.2-ounce) can sliced ripe olives, well drained
  2 cups grated sharp Cheddar cheese
  1 (0.9-ounce) bag tortilla chips

1 Spread refried beans over bottom of a large microsafe serving plate. Sprinkle chopped onion over beans. Pour the taco sauce over this layer and sprinkle with sliced olives.

2 Top with grated cheese and cover with vented plastic wrap.

3 Microcook on High Power 3-5 minutes or until cheese is melted and mixture is heated through.

4 Place tortilla chips on their edges all over the top of the mixture. The chips become ready-made scoopers positioned for serious eating.

- Serves 6-8

PEPPER PIZZA

Do you know anyone who doesn't love pizza? These individual pizzas make a nice snack or appetizer. You could cut the cooked pizzas into fourths and serve as bite-sized slices if you wish.

    4 (6-inch) corn tortillas
    1 teaspoon olive oil
    2 cloves garlic, minced
  1/2 medium green bell pepper, cut into thin strips
  1/2 medium red bell pepper, cut into thin strips
    4 slices salami, cut into thin strips
  1/2 cup sliced fresh mushrooms
  1/4 cup tomato paste
  1/2 teaspoon bottled dried Italian herbs or oregano
    4 tablespoons grated Mozzarella cheese

1   Lay the tortillas on a piece of paper toweling and place in the microwave. Microcook on High Power 3 minutes or until crisp. Remove from the oven and set aside.

2   Combine the olive oil, garlic and peppers in a small microsafe bowl. Microcook on High Power 2 minutes.

3   Add the salami, mushrooms, tomato paste, and Italian herbs to the pepper mixture. Microcook on High Power 1 1/2 minutes. Spread on top of the tortillas and sprinkle with the cheese. Place tortillas on a serving dish or individual plates and microcook on High Power 30-60 seconds or until cheese melts.

•   Serves 4

PITA PIZZA

  1 (6-inch) pita pocketbread round
  1 (4-ounce) can pizza sauce
  6 pepperoni or salami pieces, thinly sliced into strips
1/2 cup chopped fresh mushrooms
1/2 cup shredded Jack or Mozzarella cheese
    Parmesan cheese
1/2 teaspoon bottled dried Italian herb seasoning

1 Carefully pull or cut the two pieces of the pocket bread apart. Place each round on a paper plate.

2 Spread each pita round with a thin layer of pizza sauce and sprinkle on pepperoni strips, chopped mushrooms, Jack cheese, Parmesan cheese and dried Italian herbs. Microcook on High Power until cheese is bubbling 45-60 seconds. Let cool slightly before indulging.

Note: You might prefer to cut the circles into quarters before you add the toppings if you're planning to serve them as a bite sized appetizer.

● 1 pita pocket bread makes 2 servings

Pita bread makes a marvelous ready-made crust for these yummy appetizers. They can also be served as a quickly prepared lunch. For a more health conscious creation, substitute fresh vegetables for the pepperoni and use low fat cheese. Children love to make this tasty treat.

These marinated mushrooms are easy to prepare, low in calories and and are quickly consumed. If you happen to have a few left, toss them in a green salad for a special flavor accent.

MUSHROOMS À LA GRECQUE

1 pound fresh small button mushrooms	2 cloves garlic, crushed
2/3 cup extra virgin olive oil	1 bay leaf, whole
1/2 cup water	1/2 teaspoon dried thyme
1/4 cup lemon juice	1 teaspoon dried oregano
3 tablespoons minced green onion	10 black peppercorns
6 sprigs parsley, chopped	1 teaspoon salt

1 Clean mushrooms with a damp paper towel. Trim stems and place caps in a 2-quart microsafe casserole.

2 In a large microsafe bowl combine the olive oil, water, lemon juice, onion, parsley, garlic, bay leaf, thyme, oregano, peppercorns and salt. Microcook on High Power 2-4 minutes or until boiling. Continue cooking on Medium Power (50%) 3-5 minutes to combine flavors. Let stand 5 minutes.

3 Pour marinade over mushrooms and microcook on High Power 3-5 minutes, stirring every minute to rearrange the mushrooms.

4 Leave the mushrooms in the marinade and refrigerate. Drain mushrooms thoroughly and serve chilled or at room temperature with toothpicks. These will keep several weeks refrigerated.

• Makes 2-3 cups

TORTILLA PINWHEELS

For this quick and easy recipe, the microwave is used for softening cream cheese and warming the tortillas.

2 (8-ounce) packages cream cheese
1 (1-ounce) package ranch salad dressing mix
2 green onions, minced
4 (12-inch) flour tortillas
1/2 cup finely diced red bell pepper
1/2 cup finely diced celery
1 (2.2-ounce) can sliced black olives, drained

1 Place the cream cheese, dressing mix and green onions in a microsafe bowl. Microcook on High Power 2-3 minutes. Stir to combine ingredients.

2 Place a sheet of paper towel on the floor of the microwave. Layer the 4 tortillas onto the paper towel and microcook on High Power 1 minute.

3 Spread the cream cheese mixture onto the tortillas. Sprinkle with the red pepper, celery and black olives.

4 Roll tightly and wrap each tortilla roll in plastic wrap.

5 Refrigerate at least 2 hours. Remove plastic wrap, cut off the roll ends and cut the rolls into 1-inch slices.

• Makes 36 slices

The ingredients for this colorful appetizer travel well. So it's perfect for boat, cabin and RV entertaining. The presentation is really quite smashing —anywhere!

PESTO SAUCED TORTELLINI—BROCCOLI SKEWERS

1 pound tortellini	6 tablespoons olive oil
2 teaspoons olive oil	2 tablespoons green onions,
1/2 cup bottled pesto sauce	finely minced
(or your favorite recipe)	2 teaspoons dried dill weed
2 tablespoons wine vinegar	3 large stalks broccoli
1 teaspoon Dijon mustard	24 (8-inch) wooden skewers

1 Cook the tortellini in boiling salted water on the cook top according to directions on package. Drain well and immediately toss with 2 teaspoons olive oil.

2 In a small bowl, combine the wine vinegar, Dijon mustard, 6 tablespoons olive oil, minced green onion and dill weed. Whisk well and add the pesto sauce.

3 Cut bite-sized florets from the broccoli and rinse in cold water. Place the florets in a microsafe casserole, cover and microcook on High Power 3-5 minutes, or until bright green and crisp-tender. Drain and combine with the tortellini.

4 Toss the broccoli-tortellini mixture with some of the pesto dressing and then put 2-3 pieces on each of the wooden skewers.

5 Fan out the skewers on a decorative serving plate. These can be
refrigerated and then warmed slightly in the microwave
(8 skewers-High Power 30 seconds). They can also be served at
room temperature.

• Serves 8-10

POLENTA TRIANGLES

You'll be amazed at how easily your microwave cooks up smooth polenta. This make-ahead appetizer derives added crunch and flavor from a combination of vegetables. Cutting the polenta into triangles makes a nice change from the usual squares. These tasty triangles could also be served with a soup or salad.

1 cup coarse yellow cornmeal
1 envelope onion soup mix
3 cups cold water
1 (4-ounce) can mild chopped green chiles, drained
1/2 cup whole kernel corn, canned or fresh
1/3 cup jarred roasted red peppers, finely chopped
1/2 cup shredded sharp Cheddar cheese

1   In a large microsafe casserole combine cornmeal, onion soup mix and water. Microcook, covered, on High Power 20 minutes, stirring every 5 minutes. Mixture will be thick.

2   Stir in green chiles, corn and red peppers. Spread into a lightly greased 8-inch square microsafe casserole; sprinkle with cheese. Let stand at room temperature 20 minutes or until firm.

3   Cut into triangles. Serve at room temperature or microcook on High Power 30 seconds or until warm.

•   Makes 30 appetizers.

PORK MEDALLIONS
WITH THREE DIPPING SAUCES

These delectable pork medallion appetizers are always a hit at parties. This recipe is so simple, so tasty and so elegant in its presentation, I am certain you will serve it often.

　1　2-3 pound pork tenderloin
1/2　cup orange marmalade
1/2　cup bottled plum sauce
1/2　cup toasted sesame seeds

1　Place the tenderloin on a microsafe plate. Cover with vented plastic wrap and microcook on High Power, 8-9 minutes per pound. Let stand covered 5 minutes.

2　When slightly cooled, slice into thin medallions. Arrange on an attractive platter with small containers of orange marmalade, plum sauce and sesame seeds. Guests enjoy dipping and savoring the lovely pork flavor which is enhanced by the sauces and seeds.

•　Makes 18-24 medallions

This 'healthy for you' dip with spicy, exotic oriental flavors is simple to prepare thanks to the microwave and processor. Fix it and enjoy it served with fresh jicama strips and radish slices as 'scooper uppers.' You can freeze any leftovers for later use.

SESAME PEA DIP

1 1/2 cups frozen peas
   2 cloves garlic, peeled
1 1/2 tablespoons sesame oil
1 1/2 tablespoons lemon juice
1 1/2 tablespoons soy sauce
  1/4 teaspoon hot chile oil or hot pepper sauce to taste
   3 tablespoons chopped fresh cilantro
   3 tablespoons nonfat plain yogurt or sour cream
   1 cup jicama strips
   1 cup radish slices

1 Place peas in a microsafe bowl and microcook on High Power 2-4 minutes, just until hot.

2 In a food processor with the steel blade, mince the garlic. Add the peas, sesame oil, lemon juice, soy sauce, chile oil, cilantro and yogurt. Process until puréed. Transfer to a bowl and refrigerate.

3 Place in a decorative bowl and surround with jicama strips and radish slices.

• Makes about 1 1/4 cups

CRUSTY GOAT CHEESE ROUNDS

1 (8-ounce) log, goat cheese
8 butter crackers, crushed
3 tablespoons olive oil
   butter crackers
& butter lettuce leaves

1   For individual servings cut the goat cheese log into 8 rounds. Pour olive oil onto a rimmed plate and place rounds in oil to coat one side. Turn over to coat other side.

2   Dip oil-coated cheese rounds into the crushed cracker crumbs, covering both sides. Place rounds around outer edge of a large microsafe dinner plate. Microcook on Medium Power 2-3 minutes or just until warmed through and beginning to melt. On each small individual plate place a warm goat cheese round in a lettuce cup and surround with butter crackers.

3   To serve a crowd, pat the goat cheese log into a large firm circle or rectangle, brush both sides with olive oil and sprinkle with cracker crumbs. Place on a decorative microsafe serving plate. Cover loosely with waxed paper and microcook on Medium Power 2-3 minutes or until just beginning to melt. Surround with butter lettuce leaves and butter crackers and serve.

•   Serves 8-12

Turn the lights down low, light the candles and bring on this delicious treat. You and your microwave can really wow your friends with this appealing appetizer or first course. Simple, easy and yet so appealing!

Skewered appetizers always make a rather pretty presentation. These elegant bites are colorful, tasty and enhanced by the simply prepared curry dipping sauce.

SPINACH WRAPPED CHICKEN BITES WITH CURRY DIPPING SAUCE

Chicken Skewers
   2 pounds skinless boneless chicken breasts (7-8)
   2 tablespoons soy sauce
   2 tablespoons lemon juice
   1 pound fresh spinach
  24 (8-inch) wooden skewers

1 Combine soy sauce and lemon juice. Brush chicken breasts with this mixture. (Or for a simple multi-use kitchen aid, pour bottled lemon juice into a small plastic spray bottle and spritz soy sauce-brushed chicken breasts with lemon juice).

2 Place chicken breasts on a microsafe plate, cover with vented plastic wrap and microcook on High Power 4 minutes. Turn over pieces, placing less cooked portions to the outside of the plate. Re-cover and microcook on High Power 3-4 minutes or until no longer pink. Set aside and let cool. When cool cut into bite-sized chunks.

3 Wash spinach, removing stems. Place leaves in a microsafe casserole and microcook on High Power 1-2 minutes or until they just start to wilt. Set aside to cool.

4 To assemble, place a chunk of chicken at stem end of a spinach leaf. Roll over once, fold leaf in on both sides, and continue rolling around chicken. Secure end of leaf with a long wooden skewer. Refrigerate for at least 1 hour or overnight.

Curry Dipping Sauce

- 1/4 cup mayonnaise
- 1/4 cup sour cream or nonfat yogurt
- 2 teaspoons curry powder
- 2 tablespoons bottled chutney
- 1 teaspoon lemon zest (finely grated yellow skin of a lemon)

5 In a small decorative bowl combine mayonnaise, sour cream, curry powder, chutney and lemon zest. Mix until smoothly blended. Cover and refrigerate for at least 1 hour. Makes about 2/3 cup.

6 To serve, place skewered chicken pieces on a decorative serving plate. For an elegant presentation, fan them out and place the dipping sauce at the base of the fan of skewered pieces.

- Makes about 24 skewers

STICKY WINGS

Next time you need to provide a hearty appetizer for a group, try these. Perhaps doubling the recipe would be a good idea, as they are gobbled up quickly. The presentation is most appealing.

1/4 cup soy sauce	6 chicken wings, tips removed
2 tablespoons honey	and discarded, separated at joint
2 teaspoons dry sherry	1 teaspoon toasted sesame seeds
1 clove garlic, minced	1 green onion, finely minced
1/2 teaspoon minced fresh ginger	2 teaspoons minced cilantro
1/2 teaspoon sesame oil	
1/8 teaspoon Chinese five-spice powder (if available)	

1 In a zippered plastic bag, combine soy sauce, honey, sherry, garlic, ginger, sesame oil and five-spice powder. Add chicken wings and turn to coat. Turn the bag frequently. Let marinate at least 30 minutes.

2 Arrange the wing pieces in the pie plate with the thickest pieces toward the outer edge of the plate. Cover with vented plastic wrap or a plate; microcook on High Power 6 minutes. Turn plate and microcook 6 minutes longer.

3 Remove the wings from the pie plate. Microcook the remaining marinade on High Power 2-4 minutes until it becomes quite thick. Return the wings to the plate and turn them to coat with the sauce. Transfer to a serving plate and sprinkle with sesame seeds, scallions and cilantro. (Have plenty of napkins on hand).

• Makes 12 pieces

SPINACH AND SCALLOP TERRINE WITH CAPER SAUCE

Terrine

    1 pound scallops
  1/2 cup sour cream
    2 eggs
    1 shallot, chopped
    1 tablespoon white vermouth
      salt
      pepper
    2 cups whipping cream
    1 bunch spinach, well rinsed

1   In a food processor fitted with the steel knife, process scallops, sour cream, eggs, shallot, vermouth, salt and pepper. Slowly add cream while processing. Process just until smooth and thick.

2   Place spinach in microsafe casserole. Microcook on High Power 3 minutes.

3   Remove 3/4 of the scallop mixture; place in freezer. Process remaining scallop mixture with spinach, until smooth.

4   Layer white, partially frozen scallop mixture in bottom of a microsafe loaf pan. Spread spinach-scallop mixture on top.

5   Cover loaf pan with vented plastic wrap. Place loaf pan in an 8 x 12-inch microsafe baking dish. Add 1/2 inch warm water to create a water bath around the terrine and microcook on Medium Power (50%) 20-25 minutes, or until bottom of terrine appears set. Let stand covered on counter 10 minutes, then refrigerate.

Caper Sauce

3/4 cup sour cream or low fat yogurt
2 tablespoons Dijon mustard
1 teaspoon dried tarragon
1 teaspoon capers, drained
& dash cayenne pepper

6 For the caper sauce, gently combine the sour cream, Dijon mustard, tarragon, capers and cayenne pepper.

7 Loosen edges of terrine with knife and unmold onto serving platter. Cut into 8-10 slices and serve on individual plates with caper sauce.

• Makes 8-10 slices

SOUPS

Spicy Sausage Corn Chowder
Thai Chicken Coconut Soup (Gai Tom Ka)
French Onion Soup
Lemon Borscht
Pesto Soup
Shrimp and Tofu Soup
Chinese Vegetable Soup
Eggdrop Soup
Spinach Broth
Chili
Chilled Salad Soup

SOUP IS A MARVELOUS WAY to start a meal, or to be a major part of the meal.

The microwave and food processor make soup preparation fast and easy. The soups in this chapter are quite varied, ranging from Hearty Chili to Thai Chicken Coconut Soup, to Spicy Sausage Chowder, all of which will amaze and delight your friends.

If time is short, purchase a package of trimmed fresh vegetables and create your own soup using a canned low sodium chicken broth as the base. Leftover pieces of chicken, cooked grains or a few fresh or dried herbs can also be added. You can cover your creation with vented plastic wrap and microcook it on High Power, 3-4 minutes. However, if you have a 'reheat' button on your microwave, just cover, press 'reheat' and the microwave will do the rest. When you press 'reheat' the microwave figures the timing for you via a humidity sensor. When the oven turns off the soup is ready. You'll have a steaming bowl of hearty, healthy soup, spoon ready. The vegetables will be crisp-tender, and the meat and grains, which have already been cooked, will add texture and flavor.

Soups are very satisfying and their restorative powers are amazing. Why not try a soup for dessert? The Peach Soup (Dessert chapter) makes a wonderful finale to a summers' evening meal.

SPICY SAUSAGE CORN CHOWDER

2 links hot Italian sausage (8 ounces) or other spiced sausage,
    cut into 1/4-inch slices, and again into half circles
2 tablespoons chopped dehydrated onions
6 cups chicken broth
1 (11-ounce) can whole kernel corn with red and green peppers
    salt
    pepper
& fresh cilantro, optional

1   Combine sausage, onion, broth and corn in a large microsafe
    casserole. Cover with a lid or vented plastic wrap and microcook
    on High Power until it boils (about 12 minutes); then simmer on
    Medium Power (50%) 5-8 minutes.

2   Before serving, add salt and pepper to taste and garnish with fresh
    cilantro.

•   Serves 6

In this easy soup recipe the cook dictates the seasonings by the sausage that is added to these simple, basic ingredients. You will be amazed at the well seasoned, impressive potage you and your microwave produce.

This simple, hearty, country-style soup is bursting with exciting Thai flavors and is among the most often requested dishes in Thai restaurants. I served this to my Gourmet Lunch Bunch; they loved the sweet pieces of chicken and were amazed at the ease of preparation.

THAI CHICKEN COCONUT SOUP (GAI TOM KA)

1 (14-ounce) can unsweetened coconut milk
1 1/2 cups homemade or canned chicken broth
1/4 cup fresh lime juice
1 stalk fresh lemon grass, trimmed and cut into 1-inch lengths
1 2-inch piece lime peel
2 tablespoons Nam Pla (oriental fish sauce)
2 tablespoons minced fresh ginger
4 chicken breast halves, skinned, boned and cut into 1/2-inch strips
1/4 cup minced red bell pepper
1/4 cup chopped cilantro
1/8 teaspoon crushed hot red pepper flakes, or to taste

1   In a microsafe 2 or 3-quart casserole, combine coconut milk, chicken broth, lime juice, lemon grass, lime peel, fish sauce, ginger and chicken. Cover with vented plastic wrap. Microcook on High Power until chicken is cooked through, about 12-14 minutes.

2   Remove lemon grass pieces (if you wish) and strip of lime peel. Stir in red bell pepper, cilantro and crushed hot red pepper flakes. Reheat if necessary and serve immediately.

• Serves 4

FRENCH ONION SOUP

1/2 cup butter or margarine
3 pounds onions, peeled
   and thinly sliced
   (a food processor helps)
2 cloves garlic, minced
2 teaspoons sugar
6 tablespoons flour
6 cups water

2 tablespoons beef-flavored
   Instant bouillon
2 tablespoons Worcestershire sauce
1/2 teaspoon dried marjoram
1/4 teaspoon dried thyme
1/2 cup sherry
2 ounces Swiss cheese, grated

1 Place butter in a 4 or 5-quart microsafe casserole. Microcook on High Power 1 minute. Stir in onions, garlic and sugar. Cover and microcook on High Power 20 minutes, stirring occasionally.

2 Stir in flour, microcook on High Power 3 minutes.

3 Stir in water, bouillon, Worcestershire sauce, marjoram and thyme. Cover and microcook on High Power 15 minutes.

4 Stir in sherry and ladle soup into bowls. Place a French bread slice in each bowl, sprinkle with Swiss cheese and microcook on High Power until cheese is melted. Serve immediately.

• Serves 4

Many gourmands will scoff the thought of French onion soup in the microwave. Go ahead, try it. You won't believe the superb results. Let's face it, in our busy lives we don't have time for 'simmer and stir all day' recipes. Get the same results in minutes, not hours, by using your microwave.

This unusual Borscht is one I like to serve to friends. Its ease of preparation belies its delightful flavors and gorgeous presentation. To make it even more appealing, it is low in fat and calories and can be served hot or chilled.

LEMON BORSCHT

3 cups chicken or beef broth
2 cups shredded fresh beets (2 large beets, 5-6 ounces)
1/2 cup finely shredded red cabbage
6 green onions, minced
2 tablespoons fresh lemon juice (or to taste)
1 tablespoon minced fresh dill
1/2 teaspoon lemon zest (grated yellow skin of a lemon)
   salt
   cayenne pepper to taste
1/2 cup nonfat yogurt (or sour cream if you prefer)

Garnish
   lemon zest
   & dill sprigs

1 Combine the broth, beets, cabbage and half of the onions in a microsafe 3-quart casserole. Microcook covered on High Power 8-10 minutes or until vegetables are well cooked.

2 Stir in the remaining onions, lemon juice, fresh dill, lemon zest and salt to taste. Microcook for 1 minute longer. Add cayenne pepper to taste.

3 Serve chilled or hot, topped with yogurt and garnished with lemon zest and dill sprigs.

• Serves 4

PESTO SOUP

1 tablespoon butter	4 large tomatoes, peeled and chopped
1 onion, chopped	4 tablespoons prepared pesto
1 rib celery, chopped	salt
1 carrot, chopped	pepper to taste
1 tablespoon flour	2 tablespoons pine nuts
4 cups chicken broth	2 tablespoons sherry

1 Combine butter, onion, celery and carrot in a microsafe bowl. Microcook on High Power 2-3 minutes.

2 Stir in flour, add broth, mixing well.

3 Add tomatoes and pesto. Microcook on Medium Power (50%) 15 minutes. Purée in blender or processor.

4 Reheat in microwave 2-3 minutes. Add salt, pepper, pine nuts and sherry to taste.

• Serves 4

You are in luck! Commercially prepared pesto can now be found in most supermarkets. Adding other yummy vegetables, a little sherry and a few pine nuts makes this a delectable soup.

At a recent dinner party, this shrimp and tofu soup was the recipe the guests asked for.

SHRIMP AND TOFU SOUP

4 cups chicken broth
1/4 cup minced green onions
1/4 cup finely chopped carrots
1 clove garlic, minced
1 teaspoon grated fresh
  ginger root
1 teaspoon soy sauce
1/4 cup sliced mushrooms

1/2 cup cooked small shrimp
1/4 pound snow peas,
  washed and trimmed
4 ounces firm tofu
  (soy bean curd),
  cut into 1/2-inch cubes
& green onion tops, cut into
  1/2-inch lengths for garnish

1 Place broth, green onions, carrots, garlic, ginger root and soy sauce in a large microsafe bowl. Microcook on High Power 8-10 minutes.

2 Add mushrooms and shrimp. Microcook on High Power 5 minutes.

3 Add snow peas and microcook on High Power 1 minute.

4 Stir in tofu and garnish with onion tops.

Note: You can omit the shrimp and still have a lovely soup.

• Serves 4

CHINESE VEGETABLE SOUP

Leftover chicken or seafood? Add it to this low fat chunky vegetable broth for a superb oriental dinner in a dish.

1 1/2 cups chicken broth
1 1/2 teaspoons soy sauce
   1 teaspoon rice vinegar
   6 snow peas, trimmed and cut into 1/2-inch diagonals
   6 thin slices carrot
1/2 cup diced firm tofu
   1 small inside leaf bok choy, rinsed, white part diced,
      leafy part cut into thin shreds
1/2 teaspoon sesame oil
    cooked chicken or fish pieces (optional)
 & thin diagonal slices green onion, for garnish

1 Combine chicken broth, soy sauce, rice vinegar, snow peas and carrot slices in a microsafe 1-quart casserole or bowl. Cover with a lid or vented plastic wrap and microcook on High Power 3 minutes or until very hot.

2 Uncover and stir in tofu, bok choy, sesame oil and cooked chicken or fish pieces. Cover and microcook on High Power 2 minutes, or until heated through.

3 To appreciate the colorful vegetables, pour into a large shallow bowl and garnish with the scallion slices.

• Serves 1 (Recipe can easily be doubled)

Dinner guests will be impressed with the flavor AND the look of this light soup.

EGG DROP SOUP

4 cups chicken broth
1/4 cup sliced green onions
1/2 cup frozen peas
1/2 cup sliced fresh mushrooms
1 tablespoon grated fresh ginger
2 eggs, beaten

1 Pour broth into a 2-quart microsafe casserole and cover with vented plastic wrap. Microcook on High Power 8-10 minutes until stock boils.

2 Add green onions, peas, mushrooms, ginger and soy sauce to the boiling broth. Cover and microcook on High Power 1 minute.

3 Uncover and slowly drizzle beaten egg into the soup, using a circular motion. Serve.

• Serves 4

SPINACH BROTH

4 cups chicken broth
2 teaspoons lemon juice
2 cups thinly sliced fresh spinach
1 teaspoon freshly grated nutmeg
4 lemon slices, optional garnish

1   Combine broth and lemon juice in a large microsafe casserole. Cover and microcook on High Power 5 minutes.

2   Add spinach and nutmeg to hot broth, cover again and microcook on High Power 3-5 minutes or until heated through. Check for seasoning.

3   Top each serving with a lemon slice and serve.

•   Serves 4

Here is another great, low fat, satisfying soup. Chard, dandelion greens or other green leafy vegetables may be substituted.

My husband, Tom loves to make chili to eat when there are important football games on TV. This is his recipe. He likes thick chili. Add water if you like yours a little thinner.

CHILI

1/2 cup chopped onion
1 clove garlic, minced
1/4 cup chopped green pepper
1 (4-ounce) can chopped green chiles
1 pound lean ground beef
1 (16-ounce) can tomato sauce
1 (16-ounce) can whole stewed tomatoes,
    undrained and chopped
1 1/2 teaspoons salt
1-3 tablespoons chili powder
1/2 teaspoon dry mustard
1/2 teaspoon dried oregano
1 teaspoon cumin
1 teaspoon sugar
1/4 teaspoon cayenne pepper (optional)
1 (15-ounce) can kidney beans, drained

Garnish
1 cup grated Cheddar cheese
1 cup chopped onion

1 Combine onion, garlic, green pepper, chopped green chiles and ground beef in a microsafe 3 or 4-quart casserole. Cover with lid or plastic wrap and microcook on High Power 7-8 minutes or until beef is no longer pink, stirring after 4 minutes. Drain off drippings.

2 Add tomato sauce, stewed tomatoes, salt, 1 tablespoon chili powder, mustard, oregano, cumin and sugar. Cover and microcook on High Power 10 minutes, stirring after 5 minutes.

3   Taste for seasoning. Add more chili powder or optional cayenne
    pepper if you really want it hot. Add drained kidney beans and
    cover. Microcook on High Power 10-12 minutes or until beans
    are tender, stirring after 5 minutes. Serve immediately, passing
    bowls of grated Cheddar cheese and chopped onion to sprinkle
    on top.

• Serves 4-6

Here is an unusual soup for a hot summer day. Microcook one of the quick breads in the Bread chapter to serve with it. Dinner is ready, your kitchen stays cool and so do you!

CHILLED SALAD SOUP

1 teaspoon vegetable oil
4 shallots, sliced
3 cloves garlic, minced
4 cups salad greens, rinsed well and torn
2 cups milk
1 cup chicken broth
1 tablespoon oat bran
1/4 cup fresh basil, chopped (or 1 teaspoon dried)
    zest of one lemon (grated yellow skin)
& pepper to taste

1   Place oil, shallots and garlic in a 2-quart microsafe bowl. Microcook on High Power 2 minutes.

2   Add greens and stir to combine. Microcook on High Power 2-3 minutes, stirring until greens are wilted.

3   Add milk, chicken broth, oat bran, basil and lemon zest. Transfer to a food processor fitted with a steel blade. Process 2 cups at a time until smooth. Return to original container and microcook on High Power another 2-3 minutes. Chill and serve. May also be served warm if you prefer (microcook on High Power 3-4 minutes).

•   Serves 4

SALADS

Chilled Tortellini with Sun-dried Tomatoes, Cheese and Herbs

Chilled Spicy Peanut Noodles

Bean Thread Salad

Pasta Primavera Salad

California Chicken Salad

Mediterranean Spinach Salad with Fresh Mint and Pine Nuts

Mixed Greens with Warm Goat Cheese and Balsamic Vinaigrette

Warm Rice Salad in Red Pepper Cups

Warm Scallop Salad

German Potato Salad

Tarragon Chicken Vegetable Salad

SALADS IN THE MICROWAVE? Absolutely! This chapter contains a variety of
favorite salads. There are salads hearty enough for summer suppers, a
number of unusual pasta salads and several warm ones. You'll have a
repertoire equal to that of a fine restaurant!

Packaged ready-to-use fresh vegetables are available in many produce
sections of supermarkets. Microcook the rinsed vegetables, covered, on
High Power until crisp-tender. Notice how the color of the vegetables
actually intensifies after cooking. Add a light oil and vinegar dressing, a few
chopped nuts and currants and enjoy.

If you enjoy a Mexican salad served in a tortilla shell, here is a fat free trick
to use in preparing the crispy shell: Spray both sides of a flour tortilla with
nonfat cooking spray. Press the tortilla over an inverted microsafe bowl
and microcook on High Power 2-3 minutes or until crisp. Remove and
cool. Repeat, making as many shells as you need. Fill the shells with your
favorite recipe for the salad or Beef Salad Olé from my *Everyday Gourmet*
cookbook.

Try a microwave salad today. Choose a recipe from this chapter or
create your own. You'll be amazed at the results.

CHILLED TORTELLINI WITH
SUN-DRIED TOMATOES, CHEESE AND HERBS

RV, cabin and boat owners, as well as campers and picnic goers will especially like this recipe. All the ingredients are easily portable, the finished presentation is beautiful to behold and it tastes quite wonderful.

1	pound cheese tortellini, (dry or fresh) cooked in boiling salted water per package directions
1/3	cup chopped sun-dried tomatoes in oil
1/2	cup chopped fresh basil
1/3	cup crumbled blue cheese
1/3	cup pine nuts
1/3	cup bottled champagne salad dressing (or any oil and vinegar dressing)

1   Spread the pine nuts on a microsafe plate. Toast in microwave by microcooking on High Power in 2 minute intervals, stirring to prevent burning.

2   Combine cooked tortellini, sun-dried tomatoes, fresh basil and blue cheese.

3   Toss with dressing, test for seasoning, sprinkle with pine nuts and serve.

•   Serves 6-8

These spicy noodles are always a hit. Next time you want to serve an unusual salad, toss these ingredients together and arrange them on a large shallow plate or platter.

CHILLED SPICY PEANUT NOODLES

    8 ounces uncooked spaghetti, dry or fresh
    1 tablespoon salt
 1/4 cup corn oil
    3 tablespoons sesame oil
    1 teaspoon dry red pepper,
      finely crushed or powdered (or chili oil)
    3 tablespoons honey
    2 tablespoons soy sauce
    1 teaspoon salt
    2 tablespoons coarsely chopped cilantro
 1/4 cup roasted peanuts, chopped
 1/4 cup green onions, thinly sliced
    1 tablespoon toasted sesame seeds
    & cilantro leaves for garnish

1   Bring a large pot of water to boil on cook top. Add 1 tablespoon salt and 8 ounces of uncooked spaghetti. Cook as package directs or until done.

2   Combine corn oil, sesame oil and finely crushed red peppers in a microsafe bowl. Microcook on High Power 2 minutes.

3   Place honey jar (lid removed) or non-metal honey container in microwave. Microcook on High Power 1 minute to warm for easier measuring. Combine honey with soy sauce and salt. Blend well.

4   When pasta is cooked, drain but do not rinse. Combine immediately with oils and hone-soy sauce mixture. Cover and refrigerate for several hours or overnight.

5 When ready to serve, add cilantro, peanuts and green onions. Toss together, place in decorative serving bowl and sprinkle with toasted sesame seeds. Garnish with cilantro leaves.

Note: Chunks of microcooked chicken breast pieces may be added for a more substantial salad.

- Serves 8-10

The light oriental flavors of this unusual noodle salad combined with bright colorful pea pods, radishes and carrots are sure to impress your luncheon or dinner guests. The microwave eases your preparation by cooking the noodles, heating the pea pods and toasting the sesame seeds.

BEAN THREAD SALAD

1 package (3 3/4-ounces) cellophane (bean thread) noodles
1/2 teaspoon sugar
1/2 teaspoon salt
2 tablespoons sesame oil
1 tablespoon peeled and grated fresh ginger
2 cloves garlic, minced
1/3 cup rice wine vinegar
2 tablespoons white wine
3/4 cup shredded carrots
1/2 cup green onions (4-5), sliced diagonally
1/2 cup sliced radishes (5-6)
1/2 pound snow peas
1 tablespoon sesame seeds

1 Pour 3 cups water into a large microsafe bowl. Cover with vented plastic wrap and microcook on High Power 8-10 minutes or until boiling. Add noodles and microcook, uncovered, on High Power 2 minutes. Stir and microcook on High Power 2-3 minutes. Remove from oven, stir and let soak 5-10 minutes or until very soft. If water remains, drain it off. Cut the noodles into smaller pieces. Reserve and refrigerate.

2 Rinse snow peas and snip off ends. Cut snow peas in half on the diagonal and place in a microsafe bowl. Cover with vented plastic wrap and microcook on High Power 2-3 minutes, just until crisp-tender. Rinse under cold water to preserve fresh green color and to stop cooking. Reserve and refrigerate.

3 For dressing, combine the sesame oil, fresh ginger, garlic, wine vinegar and white wine in a glass jar and refrigerate.

4 Toss carrots and green onions into noodles. Pour dressing over and toss to coat. Add radishes and snow peas to mixture. Salad can be prepared as long as four hours before serving.

5 Sprinkle sesame seeds on a microsafe plate and microcook on High Power 2-3 minutes or until toasted. Sprinkle on top of the finished creation.

Note: Add 3/4 pound cooked bay shrimp or 1 cup cooked chicken shreds if you wish to make this a main course salad.

- Serves 4

When you want to serve a salad to a crowd this is a great recipe. It is healthy, beautiful, costs only pennies per serving and tastes divine. In this recipe the microwave cooks the vegetables perfectly and quickly and eliminates the need to use several pots and pans.

PASTA PRIMAVERA SALAD

Dressing
2/3 cup olive oil
1/4 cup lemon juice
1/4 cup white wine vinegar
  2 teaspoons salt
1/2 teaspoon freshly ground black pepper
  3 cloves garlic, minced
  3 tablespoons chopped fresh basil leaves
  2 tablespoons Dijon mustard

1 In a small bowl, combine olive oil, lemon juice, wine vinegar, salt, pepper, garlic, fresh basil leaves and mustard. Mix well and set aside.

Pasta Salad
1 (16-ounce) package large shell macaroni
1 pound fresh mushrooms, thinly sliced
1 pint whole ripe cherry tomatoes, stemmed
1 (6-ounce) can pitted whole black olives, drained
1 bunch green onions, thinly sliced (including green portion)
1 pound snow peas, trimmed and strings removed
4 carrots, thinly sliced
1 bunch broccoli, cut in florets
1 head cauliflower, cut in florets
  salt
& freshly ground black pepper

2 Cook macaroni in boiling salted water on cook top according to package directions. Cook until tender and drain.

3   In a large decorative salad bowl, combine macaroni, mushrooms, tomatoes, olives, green onions and snow peas. Refrigerate.

4   Place carrots, broccoli and cauliflower into individual plastic bags. Do not close bags. Place bag of carrots in microwave and microcook on High Power 3-4 minutes or until crisp-tender. Drain and plunge carrots into cold water; drain well. Repeat process for broccoli (cooking 3-4 minutes), and cauliflower (cooking 4-6 minutes).

5   Add cooked carrots, broccoli and cauliflower to the macaroni mixture and pour dressing over. Toss to combine and chill until ready to serve. Season with salt and pepper to taste.

•   Serves 12-14

Only in California would we put flowers in a salad. Actually, edible flowers are not an uncommon garnish in restaurant presentations. This main course luncheon entrée salad is beautiful to behold and has unusual seasonings.

CALIFORNIA CHICKEN SALAD

Cumin dressing
2/3 cup sour cream
1/2 cup mayonnaise
1 tablespoon ground cumin

I Combine dressing ingredients: sour cream, mayonnaise and cumin; refrigerate.

Salad
4 skinless, boneless chicken breast halves
1 head romaine lettuce, torn in bite-sized pieces
2 large ripe tomatoes, chopped
1/2 small red onion, thinly sliced
3 ounces Monterey Jack cheese, grated
1 (4-ounce) can diced green chiles
1 (2.2-ounce) can sliced black olives, drained
1/2 cup shredded jicama
1/4 cup chopped, fresh cilantro
1 ripe avocado
2 cups tortilla chips
1 cup crushed tortilla chips
chopped fresh cilantro
& nasturtium blossoms (optional garnish)

2 Place the chicken breasts on a microsafe plate, cover with vented plastic wrap and microcook on High Power 8-10 minutes or until juices run clear when pierced with a fork. Let cool and pull chicken into long shreds.

3 Gently toss chicken with the romaine, tomatoes, red onion, cheese, chiles, olives, jicama and 1/4 cup cilantro. Refrigerate for 1 hour.

4 Just before serving peel and seed the avocado, cut into bite-sized pieces and add to the salad.

5 To serve, arrange salad on a platter and surround with tortilla chips. Pour dressing over the salad and garnish with crushed tortilla chips, cilantro and nasturtium blossoms, if available.

• Serves 8

Here is a low fat spinach salad with some new flavors added. It has a nice combination of flavors and is easy to prepare, thanks to your microwave.

MEDITERRANEAN SPINACH SALAD WITH FRESH MINT AND PINE NUTS

1   pound fresh spinach
2   tablespoons fresh lemon juice
1   tablespoon chopped onion
1/8 teaspoon ground coriander
1/2 teaspoon salt
    freshly ground black pepper
1   cup nonfat yogurt or sour cream
1   tablespoon chopped fresh mint
2   tablespoons toasted pine nuts
    (microcook High Power, 2 minutes)

1   Wash spinach. Do not dry. Place in a microsafe 3-quart casserole and microcook on High Power 3-4 minutes. Drain and cool to room temperature. Chop into small pieces.

2   In a decorative serving bowl, combine the spinach, lemon juice, onion, coriander, salt and pepper. Toss the mixture. Stir in the yogurt and mix thoroughly.

3   Refrigerate at least 1 hour. Serve sprinkled with chopped mint and toasted pine nuts.

•   Serves 4

MIXED GREENS WITH WARM GOAT CHEESE AND BALSAMIC VINAIGRETTE

Everyday green salad becomes extra special with just a little help from your microwave.

1/2 cup pecan halves (or walnuts)	1 cup extra virgin olive oil
1 teaspoon brown sugar	6 cups mixed spring greens,
1/2 cup balsamic vinegar	torn into bite-size pieces
1 small clove garlic, minced	1 (11-ounce) tube goat cheese
1/2 teaspoon Dijon mustard	1/2 cup dry bread crumbs

1 Place the pecan halves on a microsafe plate. Microcook on High Power 1-2 minutes or until toasted. In a small bowl, combine the brown sugar with the balsamic vinegar. Whisk in the garlic, mustard and olive oil until well combined. Makes 1 1/2 cups.

2 Place greens in a large salad or mixing bowl. Toss with enough vinaigrette to coat well, reserving 1/4 cup dressing for later use. Evenly divide the salad among four small chilled plates and top with equal amounts of the toasted pecans.

3 Slice the goat cheese crosswise into 8 (1/4-inch thick) slices. Dip slices in bread crumbs. Drizzle 1/4 cup vinaigrette over goat cheese slices and microcook on Medium Power (50%) 1-2 minutes, heating just until warm. Using a spatula, place two slices of warm goat cheese on top of each salad and serve immediately.

• Serves 4

WARM RICE SALAD IN RED PEPPER CUPS

This wonderful salad could serve as a meatless main dish on a hot summer evening. In addition to cooking this salad, the microwave helps to keep the kitchen cool and uses very little electricity.

1/2 cup long grain rice
1 1/2 cups water
3/4 teaspoon salt
  3 tablespoons olive oil
  1 tablespoon red wine vinegar
  1 clove garlic, crushed
     freshly ground pepper
  1 large red bell pepper halved, seeded and stems discarded
1/4 cup chopped green bell pepper
1/4 cup chopped carrot
1/4 cup chopped celery
  1 green onion, trimmed and chopped
1/2 cup shredded Monterey Jack cheese (2 ounces)

1   Combine the rice, water and 1/2 teaspoon of the salt in a microsafe 2-quart casserole. Cover with a lid or plastic wrap and microcook on High Power 15 minutes. Let stand covered 5 minutes.

2   In a small microsafe bowl, whisk together the oil, vinegar, garlic, the remaining 1/4 teaspoon salt and a grinding of pepper. Lightly brush the inside and outside of the pepper halves with this vinaigrette, reserving some to toss with the rice.

3   Place the peppers, cut side down in a microsafe 2-quart casserole. Cover with a lid or plastic wrap and microcook on High Power 2 minutes. Let stand covered until ready to fill.

4   Combine the hot cooked rice with the chopped green pepper, carrot, celery, green onion and 1/4 cup of the cheese. Microcook the remaining vinaigrette on High Power 30 seconds, or until warmed through. Add to the rice mixture and combine.

5   Spoon the rice mixture into the pepper halves. Sprinkle with the remaining cheese. Microcook uncovered until heated through, about 2 minutes.

- Serves 2

Fancy restaurants have nothing on you. Using your microwave you can prepare this popular seafood salad. Would you believe it takes only 2 minutes to cook the scallops? Your dinner will be ready in no time at all.

WARM SCALLOP SALAD

Dressing
    4 tablespoons olive oil
    2 tablespoons fresh lime juice
    1 teaspoon sesame oil
  1/4 teaspoon salt

1 Whisk the olive oil, lime juice, sesame oil and salt in a small bowl.

Scallop Salad
    8 ounces bay scallops
      (about 1/2-inch in diameter, rinsed and patted dry)
  1/8 teaspoon crushed hot red pepper flakes
  1/4 cup plain yogurt or sour cream
    4 cups fresh torn lettuce
  1/4 cup thinly sliced red onion
  1/4 cup cilantro leaves
    1 small cucumber, peeled and thinly sliced
  1/4 medium red bell pepper, seeded and cut into thin slivers
    1 small ripe avocado, peeled and pitted,
      cut into 1/2-inch thick wedges
    1 tablespoon thinly sliced green onion tops

2 Arrange the scallops in a single layer on a microsafe pie plate; sprinkle with 1 tablespoon of the previously prepared dressing and the red pepper flakes. Toss to coat. Set aside.

3 Whisk the yogurt into the remaining dressing and set aside.

4   Combine the lettuce, onion and cilantro leaves in a large bowl.
    Place the cucumber and red bell pepper in another bowl.

5   Cover the scallops with plastic wrap and microcook on High
    Power 2 minutes, rotating the dish 180° halfway through cooking.
    Uncover and strain off the excess liquid. Add the scallops to the
    cucumber and red pepper mixture; add 2 tablespoons of the
    dressing and toss.

6   Add 2 tablespoons of the remaining dressing to the lettuce
    mixture and toss. Divide the lettuce between two large dinner
    plates. Mound the scallop mixture in the center and drizzle with
    any remaining dressing. Garnish the plates with the avocado slices
    and sliced green onion tops. Serve at once.

•   Serves 2

GERMAN POTATO SALAD

This traditional recipe is my friend Bobbe's family recipe that I have modified for cooking in the microwave. The flavors remain the same, but MY what a savings in time! You can prepare your traditional family favorites in 1/4 the time and in many cases without fats by using your microwave.

    3 pounds red-skinned potatoes
  1/2 cup water
    6 slices bacon
    1 onion, thinly sliced
    3 tablespoons flour
    1 cup hot water
  2/3 cup cider vinegar
  1/4 cup sugar
    2 teaspoons dry mustard
  1/2 teaspoon salt
  1/4 teaspoon freshly ground pepper
  2/3 cup grated Swiss cheese

1 Cut potatoes in half and place in a microsafe bowl. Pour in 1/2 cup water. Microcook on High Power 8-10 minutes, rearranging and testing potatoes several times. Microcook until just tender - not soft. When cool, cut into 1/2-inch slices; set aside.

2 Place bacon on microsafe bacon cooker or on a paper towel lined microsafe plate. Microcook 6 minutes or until crisp. Let cool and crumble. Pour 1/4 cup bacon drippings into a microsafe bowl.

3 Add onions to drippings and microcook on High Power 5 minutes. Mix in the flour and microcook on High Power 2 minutes. Stir well and add hot water, vinegar, sugar and mustard. Microcook 3-5 minutes stirring occasionally. Cook until smooth and thickened. Add the reserved bacon and season with salt and pepper.

4 Place the potatoes in a 2-quart microsafe casserole; pour the vinegar mixture over the potatoes and stir gently. Microcook on High Power 8-10 minutes or until bubbling and heated through.

5 Sprinkle cheese over top. Cover with plastic wrap 5 minutes or until cheese has melted. Serve warm or cold.

• Serves 6-8

Tarragon is the flavor enhancer here. The crunchy vegetables and succulent chicken combine to produce a flavorful, low fat gourmet salad.

TARRAGON CHICKEN VEGETABLE SALAD

3 skinless, boneless
    chicken breast halves
2 tablespoons
    white wine vinegar
1/3 cup olive oil
1 teaspoon salt
1/4 teaspoon freshly ground
    & black pepper

1/2 teaspoon crushed tarragon
1 cup sliced, fresh mushrooms
1 green pepper, thinly sliced
2 small tomatoes, cut in wedges
1 small cucumber, peeled and sliced
9 cups fresh spring greens
3 hard boiled eggs, quartered

1 Place 3 chicken breast halves in a microsafe dish. Cover with vented plastic wrap and microcook on High Power 7-8 minutes, or until juice is clear when pierced with a fork. Cool and pull into long shreds.

2 Combine vinegar, oil, salt, pepper and tarragon in a large salad bowl. Add chicken shreds, sliced mushrooms and sliced green pepper. Toss lightly. Cover with plastic wrap and refrigerate at least 1 hour.

3 Line 6 dinner plates with spring greens. Add tomatoes and cucumbers to chicken mixture and toss gently. Mound on top of salad greens and garnish with hard boiled egg quarters.

• Serves 6

BREADS

PEOPLE OFTEN ASK ME
why they can't bake or reheat bread in the microwave. They can; it's just knowing how. We've all reheated bread or muffins and ended up with inedible rocks. That's because we overheated them. One muffin reheats beautifully on High Power 10 seconds. A good rule to follow in reheating breads is to microcook one bread slice or one muffin on High Power *10 seconds only*. Check for warmth and cook in 5 second intervals until the desired temperature is reached. Once you master this technique you can bake your favorite muffins either in the microwave or conventionally, freeze them in a plastic zippered bag, take out only what you need for a meal and reheat them on High Power, 10 seconds. They will taste like fresh baked because, unlike a conventional oven which dries out food, the microwave keeps the moisture in.

Baking breads in the microwave requires a few utensils and techniques for perfect results. A microsafe muffin ring (preferably one with vent holes in the bottom of each cup) and a microsafe ring mold are useful tools. However, don't delay trying these recipes if you have neither of these utensils. Simply substitute 6 microsafe custard cups or cut the tops off 6 paper hot cups to use for muffin baking. You can create a ring mold by inverting a microsafe custard cup in the center of a microsafe casserole.

When baking breads in the microwave you will have better results if you elevate the muffin ring or ring mold on an inverted microsafe bowl. Because bread doughs are rather dense, more thorough penetration of the microwaves is necessary. Elevating the bread allows the necessary penetration.

As you look through the recipes you'll notice that most of the breads have a topping of spices, nuts or cheese. These toppings not only camouflage the 'whiteness' of microcooked bread but also add flavor. Tubes of buttermilk biscuits make an easy beginning for two bread ring recipes. I have also included a popular recipe for dog biscuits. That's right, dog biscuits for your favorite canine. This too is a 'tested' recipe.

CRUNCHY ORANGE MUFFINS

 2 eggs
 1 cup orange juice
 1 tablespoon orange zest (finely grated orange skin)
1/3 cup canola oil
 2 cups flour
1/3 cup sugar
 1 teaspoon baking powder
1/2 teaspoon salt
 1 cup grape nuts cereal

1 In a mixing bowl combine eggs, orange juice, orange zest and canola oil. Beat with an electric mixer until combined.

2 Add flour, sugar, baking powder, baking soda, salt and grape nuts. Stir to combine.

3 Place paper baking cups in a microsafe muffin pan or in 6 custard cups. Fill cups 2/3 full with the batter and microcook on High Power 2 1/2 to 3 minutes, testing with a toothpick for doneness. Repeat for remaining 6 muffins.

4 To reheat, microcook one muffin 15 seconds.

• Makes 12 muffins

When you hear a friend has had a sadness in the family, quickly microcook a batch of these wonderful crunchy muffins, put them on a disposable plastic plate and take them to the friend to show you care. Your visit and the muffins are guaranteed to add a bit of sunshine to their day.

Unexpected guests? Dash to your kitchen and casually whip up these 5 minute wonders. Can't get much faster than that!

CINNAMON MUFFINS

Muffins

  1 cup Bisquick baking mix
1/4 cup milk
  1 tablespoon butter, melted
    (20 seconds High Power)
  2 tablespoons sugar
1/8 teaspoon nutmeg
  1 egg
  6 cupcake baking papers

Topping

  2 tablespoons sugar
1/4 teaspoon cinnamon
  2 tablespoons butter, melted
    (30 seconds High Power)
  2 tablespoons finely
    chopped walnuts

1   Place 6 cupcake baking papers in a microsafe muffin ring. Combine the Bisquick, milk, 1 tablespoon melted butter, nutmeg, sugar and the egg. Divide the batter evenly among the 6 cups.

2   Microcook on High Power 2-2 1/2 minutes or until tops spring back when touched lightly and are no longer doughy.

3   While muffins are baking, combine topping: 2 tablespoons sugar, cinnamon and chopped walnuts. Dip tops of warm muffins into the 2 tablespoons melted butter and then into sugar-cinnamon-nut mixture.

•   Makes 6 muffins

WALNUT STREUSEL COFFEE CAKE

1 cup chopped walnuts
2 tablespoons brown sugar
1 tablespoon flour
1/2 teaspoon cinnamon
1/8 teaspoon ground mace
1/2 cup cold butter or margarine
3/4 cup sugar

3/4 cup sour cream
1 egg
1 teaspoon vanilla
1 1/2 cups flour
1 teaspoon baking powder
1 teaspoon baking soda

Coffee cakes are a nice addition to a breakfast menu. This recipe goes together quickly and takes only 8 microwave minutes to bake.

1   Combine walnuts, brown sugar, 1 tablespoon flour, cinnamon and mace until well blended.

2   With electric mixer or processor with steel knife, beat butter and granulated sugar until smooth and fluffy. Add sour cream, egg and vanilla; mix until smooth. Sprinkle 1 1/2 cups flour, baking powder and baking soda over ingredients in bowl. Stir just until blended. Spoon half the batter into a 6-cup microsafe Bundt pan or round baking dish. Sprinkle with half the nut mixture. Repeat with remaining batter and nuts.

3   Place an inverted bowl or microwave rack in your oven and place the cake pan on this to elevate it. Microcook on Medium Power (50%) 5 minutes, rotating occasionally.

4   Microcook on High Power about 3 minutes, until cake springs back when touched. Let stand 10 minutes. Serve warm.

•   Serves 6-8

ZUCCHINI MUFFINS

These great little muffins were a real hit in my cooking classes. The nutty topping adds crunch and eye appeal as well. If you are a zucchini grower, this recipe is for you! Make a double batch and freeze some to have on hand to go with your winter soups.

2/3 cup sugar	2 small zucchini, shredded
2/3 cup brown sugar	1 1/3 cup flour
6 tablespoons vegetable oil	1 teaspoon ground cinnamon
4 tablespoons butter or margarine	1 teaspoon baking soda
2 eggs	1/4 teaspoon baking powder
1/2 teaspoon vanilla	1/4 teaspoon ground allspice
1 1/2 cup chopped pecans or walnuts	1/4 teaspoon ground nutmeg
	1/2 teaspoon salt
	24 cupcake papers

1 In a mixing bowl, combine the sugars, oil, and butter. With an electric mixer, beat until fluffy. Add eggs and vanilla to bowl and beat briefly. Add 1/2 cup of nuts and the shredded zucchini. Mix until just blended. Add flour, cinnamon, baking soda, baking powder, allspice, nutmeg and salt. Mix just until flour disappears.

2 Place 6 cupcake baking papers in a microsafe muffin pan. Note: If you don't have a muffin pan, custard cups may be used. Place cupcake baking papers in 6 cups and arrange cups in a circle on a large microsafe plate. Spoon about 2 tablespoons of the mixture into each baking paper, about half full.

3 Microcook on High Power 2 minutes, rotate pan or plate after 1 minute. Microcook on Medium Power (50%) about 1 minute, or until toothpick inserted in center of muffins comes out clean. Don't be alarmed as tops of muffins will look very moist.

4 Dip tops of muffins in remaining chopped nuts and let muffins cool 5 minutes. Repeat with rest of the dough.

• Makes 24 muffins

CHEESE TOPPED BISCUIT WEDGES

These tasty wedges add a gourmet touch when served with soups and salads. You can vary this recipe by using various herbs or omitting the bacon.

3 slices bacon	1/2 cup milk
1/2 cup chopped onion	1 egg, beaten
1 tablespoon butter	1 cup grated
or margarine	sharp Cheddar cheese
2 cups Bisquick baking mix	2 tablespoons fresh minced parsley
1/4 teaspoon salt	1 tablespoon poppy seeds

1 Microcook bacon on a bacon rack or on a paper towel covered microsafe plate on High Power 3-4 minutes. Cool, crumble the bacon and set it aside.

2 Place onion and butter in a small microsafe bowl. Cook, covered on High Power 2 minutes or until transparent.

3 In a mixing bowl combine baking mix, salt, milk, egg, 1/2 cup cheese, parsley and cooked onion. Stir just until moistened.

4 Spoon mixture into a lightly greased microsafe bundt pan or ring mold. You can also improvise by placing a microsafe glass in the center of a large round microsafe casserole. Cover loosely with waxed paper and microcook on High Power 3 minutes. Sprinkle with remaining 1/2 cup cheese, crumbled bacon and poppy seeds.

5 Cook, uncovered on High Power an additional 1-2 minutes or until bread is cooked through and the cheese is melted. Let stand 5 minutes on a rack. Cut into wedges and serve warm. Individual pieces can be reheated on High Power 10 seconds.

• Makes 6-8 wedges

ORANGE NUT COFFEE CAKE

I tested this on a crowd at our church coffee hour. Many couldn't believe it was baked in the microwave. You'll like the texture and orangy tang of this coffee cake. The orange juice is an unusual addition to the spices and nuts.

Coffee Cake

1/2 cup butter or margarine	2 cups flour
1/2 cup brown sugar	1/2 teaspoon salt
1/2 cup white sugar	1 teaspoon baking soda
2 eggs	1/2 teaspoon baking powder
1/2 cup milk	2/3 cup raisins
1/2 cup frozen orange juice concentrate (do not thaw or dilute)	1/2 cup chopped walnuts

1 In a large mixing bowl, cream the butter and sugar with an electric mixer until fluffy. Add the eggs one at a time, beating after each addition.

2 Stir together the milk and orange juice concentrate. Combine the flour, salt, soda and baking powder. Add dry ingredients to the creamed mixture, alternating with the milk and orange juice mixture. Beat thoroughly 2 minutes. Fold in the raisins and nuts.

3 Spread the cake batter in a lightly greased microsafe bundt pan which has been coated with sugar. Cook on Medium Power (50%) 14 minutes. Rotate cake 1/4 turn; microcook on High Power 2-5 minutes or until set but still slightly moist on top. Let stand 10 minutes. Turn out of pan onto a serving plate.

Topping

- 1/3 cup brown sugar
- 1/2 cup chopped walnuts
- 1 teaspoon cinnamon
- 1/2 cup frozen orange juice
  concentrate (do not thaw or dilute)

4 For the topping, mix together the brown sugar, walnuts, cinnamon and orange juice concentrate. Drizzle evenly over the cake. Cool slightly and cover to preserve moistness. Serve warm or at room temperature.

- Makes 12-16 slices

Your food processor can grate the cheese and mix the batter for these yummy corn bread squares. Then pop them in your microwave for just 5 minutes.

ONION CORN BREAD SQUARES

1/2 cup chopped onion	1 tablespoon vegetable oil
2 tablespoons butter or margarine	2 ounces grated Cheddar cheese
1 cup buttermilk	1 cup cornmeal
2 eggs	1 cup flour
2 tablespoons sugar	1 1/2 teaspoon baking powder
	1/2 teaspoon salt

1   Place onion and butter in a small microsafe bowl. Microcook on High Power until onion is golden, 2-4 minutes, stirring after 2 minutes.

2   In a mixing bowl, combine buttermilk, eggs, sugar, oil and half the cheese. Mix until smooth. Add onion mixture, cornmeal, flour, baking powder and salt. Stir to combine.

3   Spoon batter into a greased 8-inch square microsafe baking dish. Microcook on High Power 3-5 minutes or until mixture is set and springs back when touched. Rotate dish 1/4 turn every 2 minutes.

4   Sprinkle reserved cheese over cornbread. Let stand uncovered 5 minutes. Cut into squares; serve warm.

•   Makes 16 squares

CHILE CHEESE CORNBREAD

This cornbread recipe has the added texture and color of corn and green chiles. It has a marvelous flavor and is quickly and easily prepared.

  2 eggs
  1 (8-ounce) can whole kernel corn, drained
  1 tablespoon baking powder
  1 cup sour cream
1/2 cup melted butter
  1 cup corn meal
  1 teaspoon salt
  1 (4-ounce) can diced green chiles
  1 cup grated Monterey Jack cheese

1 Beat eggs; add corn, baking powder, sour cream, butter, corn meal and salt. Stir to combine and pour half the batter into a greased 8-inch square microsafe baking dish. Place chiles on top of the batter and sprinkle with half the cheese.

2 Spread remaining batter over the top and microcook on High Power 10 minutes, rotating dish one quarter turn several times.

3 Sprinkle remaining cheese over top and let stand 5 minutes before cutting into squares.

• Makes 16 squares

The black poppy seeds add color contrast and crunch to these delectable bites. Rather high in fat content—try not to eat too many!

CHEDDAR POPPY SEED BREAD

1/2 cup butter, melted (High Power 30 seconds)
1 cup (4-ounces) grated Cheddar cheese
1 1/2 cups flour
1/2 teaspoon salt
1/8 teaspoon cayenne pepper
1 tablespoon dehydrated minced onion
3 tablespoons poppy seeds

1   Combine melted butter, cheese, flour, salt, cayenne pepper, onion and 2 tablespoons poppy seeds. Stir until well mixed.

2   Press mixture into an 8 x 8-inch or round microsafe casserole. Press remaining 1 tablespoon poppy seeds evenly over top.

3   Microcook on High Power 5 1/2-6 minutes or until firm and no longer doughy. While hot, cut into squares or wedges. Serve warm or cold as an appetizer or as an accompaniment to soup or salad.

•   Makes 16-24 squares or wedges

OLIVE CHEESE FLATBREAD

You'll like this easy
recipe. It makes a
great accompaniment
to soup or salad.

1 1/2 cups Bisquick baking mix
   1 teaspoon dried sage
3/4 cup milk
   3 tablespoons olive oil
1/2 cup grated Cheddar cheese
   1 (2.2-ounce) can sliced olives, drained
1/2 teaspoon garlic salt

1 In a mixing bowl combine the baking mix and sage. Stir in the milk until well combined.

2 Grease an 8 or 9-inch microsafe plate with 1 tablespoon olive oil. Place a microsafe glass in the center of the plate. Spread the dough evenly on the plate, surrounding the glass. Pour the remaining 2 tablespoons olive oil over the dough and spread to cover evenly.

3 Microcook, uncovered, on High Power 3 minutes. Sprinkle with cheese, olives and garlic salt. Microcook on High Power 1 minute or until the cheese is melted.

4 Let stand on a rack to cool for 5 minutes. Cut into wedges and serve warm.

• Makes 8-12 wedges

Here's a great bread recipe that starts with a tube of refrigerator biscuits. I prepared this bread ring on a recent TV cooking show. The stage crew couldn't believe how quickly it was prepared and did they devour it after the filming!

ITALIAN BISCUIT RING

1/2 cup grated Parmesan cheese
1/2 teaspoon paprika
1/2 teaspoon bottled dried Italian herb seasoning (or dried oregano)
1/8 teaspoon garlic powder

1/8 teaspoon onion powder
1/4 cup butter, melted (30 seconds High Power)
1 (7.5-ounce) tube refrigerator buttermilk biscuits

1 Toss together the cheese, paprika, Italian seasoning, garlic and onion powder.

2 Open tube of biscuits and separate circles. Cut the biscuits in half. Dip these half moon shaped dough pieces in melted butter and roll to coat in the cheese mixture.

3 Arrange biscuit pieces in a microsafe ring mold or in a cake dish with an inverted custard cup in the center. Microcook on High Power 2-2 1/2 minutes or until biscuits spring back when touched. Let cool slightly.

4 Invert onto serving platter. Serve immediately.

5 If there are any remaining pieces they can be reheated in the microwave on High Power 10 seconds.

• Makes 20 small biscuit pieces

ORANGE CINNAMON BREAKFAST ROLLS

1/4 cup brown sugar
1/4 cup frozen orange juice concentrate (undiluted)
1/3 cup chopped nuts
1/2 teaspoon cinnamon
1/4 cup butter, melted (30 seconds on High Power)
  1 (7.5-ounce) tube refrigerator buttermilk biscuits

1 Combine the brown sugar, frozen orange juice concentrate, nuts and cinnamon in a shallow bowl.

2 Open the tube of biscuits and separate into circles. Cut the biscuits in half. Dip these half moon shaped dough pieces in melted butter and roll to coat in the orange-cinnamon mixture.

3 Arrange biscuit pieces with curved edge conforming to side of ring mold (or in a cake dish with an inverted custard cup in the center). Microcook on High Power 2-2 1/2 minutes or until biscuits spring back when touched. Let cool slightly.

4 Invert onto serving platter. Serve immediately.

Note: If there are any remaining pieces they can be reheated in the microwave on High Power 10 seconds.

• Makes 20 small rolls

This recipe also gets a quick start with a tube of buttermilk biscuits. It's simple to prepare; in fact children can experience instant success preparing these as a birthdaty treat for Mom or Dad on their birthdays.

Next time you want to serve bread to a group, fix this delectable loaf and watch it disappear. The towel absorbs excess moisture and the microwave's speedy cooking has it table ready in just 3 minutes.

BASIL CHEDDAR FRENCH BREAD

1 large baguette sour dough French Bread
1/2 cup butter
1 cup finely grated Cheddar cheese
2 cloves garlic, crushed
3 tablespoons chopped fresh basil or 1 tablespoon dried basil
1 tablespoon dehydrated chopped onion

1   Place French bread on a dish towel or napkin, large enough to cover it completely. Slice bread on an angle in 1/2-inch slices, leaving bottom crust intact.

2   In a small microsafe bowl, microcook the butter on High Power 20 seconds or until slightly melted. Stir in the cheese, crushed garlic, basil and dehydrated onion to make a paste.

3   Spread the cheese mixture between the slices of bread. Wrap the loaf in the towel and twist the ends shut.

4   Just before serving, microcook on High Power 2-3 minutes or until the bread is warm and cheese slightly melted. Pull apart slices to serve.

•   Makes 12-16 slices

PUMPKIN BREAD

1 cup sugar
1 cup mashed cooked pumpkin
   (fresh or canned)
1/3 cup vegetable oil
1/2 cup buttermilk
2 eggs

1 2/3 cups flour
1 teaspoon baking soda
3 1/2 teaspoons pumpkin pie spice
1/2 teaspoon salt
1 cup chopped nuts

At our house we enjoy this moist bread any time of year. It will stay fresh if wrapped in foil and kept refrigerated. Why not make a double batch and freeze some for your Fall entertaining?

1   Blend sugar, pumpkin, oil, buttermilk and eggs in a mixing bowl. Add the flour, soda, pumpkin pie spice, salt and 3/4 cup chopped nuts. Beat at medium speed 1-2 minutes, until just blended.

2   Sprinkle 1/4 cup chopped nuts in a 6-cup microsafe ring mold or an 8-inch square microsafe baking dish. Sprinkle a little pumpkin pie spice over the nuts.

3   Fill mold with mixture. Place the mold on a rack or inverted microsafe bowl in the microwave. Microcook on Medium Power (50%) 13-15 minutes, turning if it appears to be cooking unevenly.

4   When bread starts to pull away from the sides of the mold, it is done. Let stand 15 minutes before unmolding.

•   Makes 10-12 slices

It's rather difficult to taste test this recipe. I tasted one, but how would I know if they were good? Our daughter Lynn and her husband Diego have a lab named Drake, and he loves these biscuits. Guess you will have to bake them and serve them to your dog. A friend's special pet would love a bag of these at Christmas or any time.

DOG BISCUITS

2 cups whole wheat flour
1 egg
1/2 cup beef or chicken broth
2 tablespoons wheat germ

1/2 teaspoon garlic salt
1/2 teaspoon onion salt
1/2 teaspoon garlic powder

1   Place flour in bowl, add egg and enough broth to moisten. Add wheat germ, garlic salt, onion salt and garlic powder.

2   Roll dough into a ball. Sprinkle flour on a board and roll dough 1/2-inch thick. Using either a heart or dog bone shaped cookie cutter, or a knife, cut into shapes appealing to a dog.

3   Place 10 on a large microsafe platter, placing biscuits around outer edge. Microcook on High Power 8-9 minutes or until firm. Repeat with remaining biscuits.

•   Makes 20 biscuits

VEGETABLES

Potatoes Au Gratin

Potatoes and Mushrooms in Lemon Cream

Chinese Style Broccoli

Creamy Whipped Potatoes and Cabbage

Broccoli Timbale with Sweet and Sour Beet Sauce

Cauliflower and Tomatoes

Ratatouille

Cranberry Glazed Baby Carrots and Snow Peas

Marinated Red Onions

Vegetable Polenta Pie

Cranberry Baked Beans

Sweet Potatoes with Curried Onion Topping

Asparagus with Sweet Red Pepper Sauce

Orange Zested Carrots Grand Marnier

Sesame Snow Peas

NUTRITIONISTS HAVE PROVED that microcooked vegetables retain more

vitamins and minerals than vegetables cooked by any other method. Shorter cooking times plus no additional moisture results in fewer nutrients being drained away in excess cooking liquid. You will find that some vegetables are even brighter in color after cooking than they were fresh. Another nice feature of microwave vegetable cooking is that the vegetables can be served in the same container in which they were cooked.

When preparing whole vegetables such as potatoes, acorn squash or yams, pierce them several times before microcooking. This will release the steam which forms during cooking and will prevent them from exploding. For specific cooking times, refer to the instruction book that came with your microwave oven. Most vegetables should be cooked on High Power 6-7 minutes per pound. A good rule to follow is to undercook, stir, check for doneness, then microcook in 30 second intervals until the vegetable is cooked to your liking.

For a quick healthy lunch or appetizer try fresh microcooked-chilled vegetables dipped in Versatile Vegetable Sauce (see index). If you are planning to cook a 10-ounce package of frozen vegetables remove the outer wrapper and place the box of frozen vegetables upright in the microwave. Placing the box upright allows more microwaves to penetrate the frozen vegetables. Microcook on High Power 5 minutes. Vegetables will be cooked and ready to serve. Look, no bowl to wash!

POTATOES AU GRATIN

1/4 cup butter
2 pounds yellow onions, sliced
  (use 2 mm processor blade)
2 pounds russet potatoes,
  peeled and sliced
  (use 2 mm processor blade)

1 teaspoon freshly grated nutmeg
  salt
  white pepper
1 1/2 cups grated Swiss cheese
1 1/2 cups milk

1 Place butter in a microsafe round 2-quart casserole or soufflé dish.
  Microcook on High Power 1 minute or until melted. Add onions,
  stir to coat, cover and microcook on High Power until onions are
  lightly browned in spots, about 25 minutes. Stir several times while
  cooking. Remove onions and set aside.

2 Combine potatoes, nutmeg, salt and pepper and toss to coat
  evenly. Arrange half of the potato slices in the previously used
  casserole or soufflé dish and top with half the onions. Sprinkle with
  half of the cheese. Repeat layering of potato slices and onions.

3 Pour milk into a microsafe bowl and microcook on High Power
  1 1/2 minutes. Pour evenly over potato-onion layers. Sprinkle
  with remaining cheese.

4 Cover with vented plastic wrap and microcook on High Power
  18-20 minutes or until potatoes are fork tender.

• Serves 8-10

Fine restaurants serve yummy au gratin potatoes; now you can too. If you have a processor, you'll find it easy to slice the onions and potatoes. The microwave carmelizes the onions beautifully without much watching and then cooks the potatoes, cheese and onions to perfection.

This rich potato dish is a nice accompaniment to barbecued meat.

POTATOES AND MUSHROOMS IN LEMON CREAM

3 medium potatoes,
  (about 1 pound)
  pared and sliced 1/4-inch thick
1 cup cream
2 strips lemon peel
1 clove garlic, peeled, left whole

1/4 pound mushroom caps,
  sliced thin
1/4 teaspoon salt
1 tablespoon
  minced fresh parsley
  & freshly ground pepper

1 Soak potato slices in cold water 30 minutes.

2 Place the cream, lemon zest and garlic in a microsafe 2-quart casserole. Microcook on High Power 7-9 minutes until thickened and reduced by half. Remove and discard the lemon zest and garlic.

3 Blot potato slices with paper towels. Combine potatoes, mushroom slices, cream mixture and salt in a microsafe 8-inch square baking dish. Microcook on High Power 10-12 minutes, or until potatoes are cooked through. Stir several times while cooking.

4 Stir in the parsley and pepper, cover with plastic wrap and microcook on High Power 2 minutes. Let stand 3 minutes. Taste and adjust seasoning. Serve hot.

• Serves 4

CHINESE STYLE BROCCOLI

1 1/4 pound broccoli florets
   1 tablespoon peanut oil
   1 tablespoon sesame oil
 1/4 teaspoon salt
   2 teaspoons soy sauce
 1/2 tablespoon brown sugar

1   Soak broccoli in cold water 15 minutes. Drain.

2   Place broccoli in a microsafe bowl, cover with vented plastic wrap and microcook on High Power 4 minutes. Let stand, covered 2 minutes. Drain liquid.

3   Measure peanut and sesame oils into a microsafe bowl; microcook on High Power 2 minutes. Add broccoli, salt, soy sauce and brown sugar. Toss to blend flavors.

•   Serves 4

The produce sections in most grocery stores are making our lives even simpler by providing small bags of vegetables, cut, trimmed and ready to cook. These are perfect for the microwave chef. If time is of the essence, buy a bag of broccoli florets and add these few ingredients for a tasty vegetable treat.

CREAMY WHIPPED POTATOES AND CABBAGE

This is a modern version of the Irish Colcannon. It makes a perfect accompaniment for your St. Patrick's Day Corned Beef Dinner. This tasty, make-ahead whipped potato recipe is easy to prepare in the microwave and the unusual presentation makes it even more intriguing.

1 large head cabbage
4 medium-size potatoes, peeled and cubed
1/2 cup water
1/2 cup milk
6 tablespoons butter
1 medium onion, chopped
1/2 teaspoon salt
1/4 teaspoon pepper
6 green onion tops, thinly sliced

1 Wash and trim 8 nice outer cabbage leaves. Shred enough remaining cabbage to make 4 cups. Set aside.

2 Place potatoes in a microsafe casserole. Add water and cover. Cook on High Power 7-12 minutes or until fork tender, stirring once halfway through cooking. Let stand covered 3 minutes.

3 In another microsafe casserole, combine onion and 2 tablespoons butter. Cook on High Power 1-2 minutes. Stir in shredded cabbage. Cover and microcook on High Power 7-13 minutes or until cabbage is tender, stirring once halfway through cooking. Let stand covered 3 minutes.

4 In a small microsafe bowl, combine the milk with 4 tablespoons butter. Microcook on High Power 1 minute; set aside.

5 Mash the potatoes. Blend in the heated milk and butter. Add salt and pepper to taste. Stir in the cooked cabbage.

6 To serve, spoon the potato-cabbage mixture into each of the cabbage leaves. Sprinkle with green onion. If making ahead and reheating, keep in a covered casserole and reheat on High Power 3-4 minutes, stirring once; then spoon into cabbage leaf cups and serve.

- Serves 8

People are continually asking me for microwave broccoli recipes. This one is most elegant, and would be a great addition to a holiday dinner. A fast fat free way to enjoy broccoli is to cook it until crisp-tender and top with a dollop of Versatile Vegetable Sauce (see Sauce chapter).

BROCCOLI TIMBALE
WITH SWEET AND SOUR BEET SAUCE

Sweet and Sour Beet Sauce

    1 (11-ounce) can beets
    1 teaspoon cider vinegar
 1/4 teaspoon salt
       freshly ground black pepper
  & pinch sugar

1 Drain beets and reserve juice. Place beets in processor bowl fitted with steel blade. Process until smooth. Place in a microsafe bowl.

2 To the puréed beets, add vinegar, salt, pepper and sugar. Taste and adjust seasonings.

3 Just before serving, microcook on High Power 2-3 minutes. Thin the puréed mixture with remaining beet juice if too thick.

Broccoli Timbales

1/2 pound fresh broccoli (about 2 cups)
  4 eggs
3/4 cup cream
  & salt to taste

1 Wash and trim broccoli. Thinly slice stems and combine with florets in a microsafe bowl. Cover with vented plastic wrap and microcook on High Power 4 minutes or until soft.

2 Purée in food processor. Add eggs, cream and salt. Process briefly.

3 Lightly oil 8 ramekins or custard cups. Place 1/4 cup of broccoli mixture in each cup and cover each one with plastic wrap.

4 Place cups in microwave in a large circle. Microcook on High Power 3-5 minutes or until set.

5 Microcook Sweet and Sour Beet Sauce 1-2 minutes or until warmed. Spoon 2-3 tablespoons of the sauce onto each dinner plate, platter or first course plate. Unmold timbales on top of the sauce, (or you may unmold the timbales and gently spoon the sauce around them).

• Serves 8

This lovely vegetable combination will add great taste and a color accent to any meal. Eliminate the bacon to make it a zero-fat recipe.

CAULIFLOWER AND TOMATOES

2 cups cauliflower florets
2 green onions, sliced (including green part)
2 tablespoons water
1 medium tomato, chopped
2 slices bacon
1/2 teaspoon dried basil, crushed
1/8 teaspoon salt

1   In a microsafe casserole, combine cauliflower, onions and water. Cover and microcook on High Power 5-7 minutes or until cauliflower is crisp-tender. Drain well.

2   Place bacon on a plate lined with paper towel and microcook on High Power 2-3 minutes. Crumble and reserve.

3   Combine the tomato, bacon, basil and salt. Toss with cauliflower mixture.

•   Serves 4

RATATOUILLE

This classic vegetable dish is so simple to prepare in the microwave. Because it can be served hot or cold, it makes a nice picnic accompaniment.

1 medium eggplant, peeled and diced	1 teaspoon salt
1 medium onion, thinly sliced	1 clove garlic, minced
4 tablespoons olive oil	1/4 teaspoon pepper
1 green pepper, sliced	1/2 teaspoon oregano
1 medium zucchini, sliced or 1 pound fresh tomatoes peeled and cooked	1 (16-ounce) can stewed tomatoes
	1 tablespoon chopped parsley

1   Combine eggplant, garlic, onion and oil in a large microsafe casserole. Cover with vented plastic wrap and microcook on High Power 4 minutes.

2   Stir in green pepper and zucchini.

3   Combine salt, pepper, oregano, tomatoes and parsley. Pour over vegetables. Cover with plastic wrap and microcook on High Power 8-10 minutes. Let stand covered 5 minutes.

4   May be served hot or cold.

•   Serves 6-8

Wow! What a
statement these
orange and green
veggies make!
The cranberry glaze
really makes this
company fare.

CRANBERRY GLAZED BABY CARROTS AND SNOW PEAS

3 pounds baby carrots, peeled and trimmed	1/3 cup brown sugar
1/2 pound snow peas, trimmed	1 1/2 tablespoons lemon juice
3 tablespoons butter or margarine	salt
3/4 cup whole berry cranberry sauce	& freshly ground black pepper

1   Place baby carrots in a 2-quart microsafe casserole. Cover and microcook on High Power 12 minutes, or until crisp-tender. Drain and run under cold water to stop the cooking. Carrots may be refrigerated. Bring to room temperature before continuing.

2   Place the snow peas in a microsafe bowl, cover, and microcook on High Power 2 minutes or until crisp-tender. Drain and cool.

3   Prepare glaze by combining the butter, cranberry sauce, brown sugar, lemon juice and salt in a microsafe bowl. Microcook 2-4 minutes stirring occasionally, until heated through. Season with salt, pepper and more lemon juice, if needed.

4   Combine carrots, snow peas and glaze. Stir well and microcook on High Power 3-5 minutes or to serving temperature.

•   Serves 10-12

MARINATED RED ONIONS

2 cups water
2 cups white wine vinegar
1 cup sugar
3 large red onions, thinly sliced

1 Combine water, vinegar and sugar in a large microsafe bowl. Microcook on High Power 10-12 minutes.

2 Add sliced onions to the liquid. Cool, cover and refrigerate 24 hours before serving. Store in refrigerator up to 4 weeks.

• Makes about 4 cups

If you like onion sandwiches, here is the perfect recipe. Use the thin slicing blade on your processor for easy preparation. These can be added to sandwiches, salads, or used with other ingredients on crackers for a 'Quick Fix' appetizer. A few of these make a marvelous addition to bagels with cream cheese. Take a jar as a hostess gift next time you visit friends. Give them the recipe too!

This meatless entrée can be prepared fat-free by eliminating the cheese or using a nonfat cheese. Recipes calling for 'a can of' usually don't impress me. This one calls for '3 cans of' and it's great! This is an ideal recipe for your next boat outing or RV trip! We have neither a boat nor an RV and love it for a fast fix dinner.

VEGETABLE POLENTA PIE

Crust

1 1/4 cup water
1 teaspoon salt

1 teaspoon chili powder
1/2 cup cornmeal

Filling

1 (15-ounce) can chili con carne
1 (2.2-ounce) can sliced ripe olives, drained
1 (11-ounce) can whole kernel corn, drained
1/2 cup chopped green pepper

1/2 cup chopped onion
1 teaspoon salt
1/8 teaspoon garlic powder
1 cup grated sharp Cheddar cheese
& parsley or cilantro sprigs

1   Combine water, salt, chili powder and cornmeal in a microsafe pie plate or shallow casserole. Microcook 4 minutes or until thick and stiff, stirring occasionally. Spread evenly over bottom of pie plate.

2   Combine chili con carne, ripe olives, corn, green pepper, onion, salt and garlic powder. Spread mixture over previously prepared crust. Cover loosely with waxed paper and microcook on High Power 6-7 minutes or until heated through. Sprinkle cheese over top and let stand 2-3 minutes for cheese to melt.

3   Cut into pie shape wedges and top with a parsley or cilantro sprig.

•   Serves 4-6

CRANBERRY BAKED BEANS

1 (16-ounce) can whole berry cranberry sauce
1 (16-ounce) can pork and beans, drained
1 (28-ounce) can baked style beans with brown sugar
1 cup finely chopped onion
4 teaspoons dry mustard

1   Place cranberry sauce in a large microsafe casserole. Break up with a fork. Add beans, onions and dry mustard. Stir to blend in mustard and cover with lid or plastic wrap.

2   Microcook on High Power 20-22 minutes or until flavors have blended. Stir every 10 minutes.

3   Let beans stand, covered for 5 minutes. The sauce will thicken if beans are refrigerated. Can also be served cold.

•   Serves 8

Baked beans never tasted this great! Your family and friends will never know the secret of this '3 can' microwave recipe unless you tell them!

This is a fabulous taste sensation, but the presentation makes it even more unusual.

SWEET POTATOES WITH CURRIED ONION TOPPING

2 sweet potatoes
(about 8-10 ounces each)
peeled and halved lengthwise
2 cups coarsely chopped onion
2 tablespoons butter,
cut into small pieces
1 1/2 teaspoons curry powder
1/2 teaspoon ground cumin seed

1 tablespoon dried currants
or raisins
salt
freshly ground pepper
1/2 cup plain nonfat yogurt
or sour cream
1 tablespoon minced cilantro
or parsley

1 Arrange potatoes, cut side down on a microsafe plate. Cover with vented plastic wrap and microcook on High Power 7-8 minutes, or until the potatoes are evenly tender, turning the dish 180° once. Let stand covered while cooking the onions.

2 Spread the onions in a microsafe 3-quart casserole. Dot with butter. Cover with a lid or vented plastic wrap and microcook on High Power 5 minutes.

3 Stir in curry powder and cumin until well blended. Re-cover and microcook on High Power 5 minutes.

4 Stir in currants; cover and microcook on High Power 2-3 minutes or until the onions are tender.

5 Place the potatoes on individual dinner plates. Spoon the onions on top. Microcook on High Power I minute per plate just to heat up the potatoes. Sprinkle with salt and pepper. Place a spoonful of yogurt on each hot sweet potato half and sprinkle with cilantro or parsley.

• Serves 4

ASPARAGUS WITH SWEET RED PEPPER SAUCE

If you want bright green, crisp-tender asparagus with all the nutrients retained in the spears, not in the water you throw out, cook it in your microwave. The red pepper sauce in this recipe enhances the fresh flavor of this favorite vegetable and takes it out of the ordinary.

1 pound fresh asparagus
2 large sweet red bell peppers, cored and seeded
    (or 1 cup jarred roasted red peppers)
2 garlic cloves, minced
2 tablespoons olive oil
2 teaspoons red wine vinegar
1/4 cup fresh basil leaves or 1 tablespoon dried basil leaves
1/2 teaspoon salt

1   Snap tough ends off asparagus. Place in a spoke like fashion on a large microsafe plate or platter, tender tips toward center of plate and cover with vented plastic wrap. Set aside.

2   Coarsely chop peppers and place them in a microsafe bowl with the garlic and oil. Cover with vented plastic wrap. Microcook on High Power 10 minutes, stirring midway through cooking. Purée pepper mixture in a food processor along with vinegar, basil, salt and pepper. Set aside and keep warm.

3   Microcook the prepared asparagus on High Power 4-6 minutes, until bright green and crisp-tender. Let stand 3 minutes.

4   Spoon sauce on a platter; arrange asparagus on sauce. If desired, garnish with strips of red bell pepper and fresh basil leaves.

•   Serves 4

ORANGE ZESTED CARROTS GRAND MARNIER

1 pound carrots, peeled and sliced diagonally
3 tablespoons water
3 tablespoons Grand Marnier
1 tablespoon orange juice
1/2 teaspoon cornstarch
1 teaspoon orange zest (grated orange skin)
3/4 teaspoon salt
& freshly ground black pepper

1 Place carrots in a small microsafe casserole. Add water, cover and microcook on High Power 7 minutes. Drain liquid.

2 Combine Grand Marnier, orange juice and cornstarch in a small microsafe bowl. Stir until cornstarch is dissolved. Stir into carrots, along with orange zest, salt and pepper. Cover and microcook on High Power 2 minutes or until mixture is slightly thickened.

• Serves 4

Next time you're searching for a colorful vegetable to brighten a dinner plate, search no more! Here's one you'll like.

Your microwave is the answer to cooking these crisp-tender snow peas. Another easy yet impressive recipe to serve your family and friends.

SESAME SNOW PEAS

    6 ounces fresh or frozen/thawed
       snow peas, strings removed
    1 teaspoon vegetable oil
    1 teaspoon sesame seeds
  1/2 teaspoon sesame oil
      salt
    & freshly ground pepper

1   Place snow peas, vegetable oil, sesame seeds and sesame oil in a microsafe glass pie plate or shallow casserole. Toss to coat the peas with the mixture and spread evenly in the dish. Cover with vented plastic wrap and microcook on High Power just until the snow peas are crisp-tender, about 1 minute.

2   Season to taste with salt and pepper, serve hot.

•   Serves 2

GRAINS AND PASTA

Orzo with Sun-dried Tomatoes and Pine Nuts

Creamy Apricot Pecan Brown Rice

Sherried Brown Rice with Mushrooms

Wild Rice with Currants, Mushrooms and Pine Nuts

Orange Bulgur Pilaf

Savory Couscous

Barley with Almonds, Peanuts and Raisins

Cheese Polenta with Provençal Sauce

Polenta with Ricotta and Dried Fruit

Irish Oatmeal with Raisins

Lentils

Grilled Portobello Mushrooms on Warm Lentils with Mint Vinaigrette

Manicotti

GRAINS HAVE BEEN AROUND since the beginning of time. What's new is an easy, nutrient-saving way to prepare them. You don't save a great deal of time preparing them in the microwave, but they are healthy and quite simple to fix.

You will find some unique and tasty recipes in this chapter. Orzo with Sun-dried Tomatoes, Savory Couscous and Creamy Apricot Pecan Brown Rice are really wonderful. The two polentas are especially easy, as you will not have to stir them constantly as you would on top of the stove.

When you prepare a grain recipe, make a double batch, serve with a meal and freeze the rest in a plastic zipper freezer bag. When you need a side dish to accompany a grilled piece of fish or chicken, pour several servings of grain into a microsafe bowl and reheat to serving temperature. Talk about fast, easy and tasty! The microwave retains the moisture in grains so they always taste fresh cooked when reheated.

I recommend that you cook pasta in boiling salted water on the cook top, as it takes the microwave a longer period of time to boil the large volume of water needed. While the pasta is cooking, you can prepare the pasta sauce in the microwave.

ORZO WITH SUN-DRIED TOMATOES AND PINE NUTS

1 (10-ounce) can chicken broth
3 cups water
1 cup orzo (small rice-shaped pasta)
1 tablespoon pine nuts
1/4 cup sun-dried tomatoes
   in oil, chopped
2 tablespoons oil
   from sun-dried tomatoes

1 tablespoon grated fresh
   Parmesan cheese
2 tablespoons chopped
   fresh parsley
   salt
& pepper

This small rice-shaped pasta is fancied up in this recipe. It's a nice change from boiled rice or potatoes and can be frozen.

1 Pour chicken broth and water in a large microsafe bowl or casserole, cover with vented plastic wrap and microcook on High Power for approximately 6 minutes or until boiling.

2 Add orzo to the boiling broth and microcook, uncovered, on High Power for 8-9 minutes, or until tender.

3 Place pine nuts, tomatoes and oil from the sun-dried tomatoes in a microsafe bowl and microcook on High Power 1 minute.

4 Drain the orzo and mix in pine nut/tomato mixture along with the grated cheese, chopped parsley, salt and pepper.

• Serves 4 (can be frozen)

CREAMY APRICOT PECAN BROWN RICE

Many people are very fond of brown rice. This nonfat recipe is healthy, easy to prepare in your microwave and freezes well.

2 1/4 cups water
1 cup quick-cooking enriched brown rice
1 cup sliced mushrooms
3/4 cup sliced onions
3/4 cup chopped pecans
1/4 teaspoon garlic powder
1/4 teaspoon salt
freshly ground black pepper
4 dried apricots, diced
1/2 cup apricot jam

1 Heat the water in a 3-quart microsafe casserole dish in the microwave on High Power 5 minutes and remove.

2 Add the rice, mushrooms, onions, pecans, garlic powder, salt, pepper and dried apricots. Cover with vented plastic wrap and microcook on High Power 8 minutes. Stir, re-cover and microcook on High Power another 7 minutes.

3 Stir in the apricot jam and reheat to serving temperature on High Power 2-3 minutes.

• Serves 4-6

SHERRIED BROWN RICE WITH MUSHROOMS

2 1/2 cups water
1/2 teaspoon salt
1 cup uncooked brown rice
2 stalks celery, diced
1/2 medium onion, chopped

1 cup sliced fresh mushrooms
1/4 cup sherry
1/2 cup blanched slivered almonds
1/2 cup sour cream or nonfat yogurt
1 teaspoon orange zest
(finely grated orange skin)

1 Pour water, salt and rice into a 3-quart microsafe casserole or bowl. Cover with vented plastic wrap and microcook on High Power 6-10 minutes or until boiling. Continue to cook on Medium Power 25-30 minutes or until most of the liquid is absorbed.

2 Place celery, onion, mushrooms and sherry in a microsafe bowl. Cover and microcook on High Power 4-5 minutes or until tender.

3 Stir vegetable mixture, almonds, sour cream and orange zest into rice. Microcook on High Power until heated through, about 3 minutes.

• Serves 10-12

The nutty brown color and wonderful textures and flavor of this brown rice recipe make a big hit with company. Freeze the leftovers and just reheat in your microwave for a mid-week taste treat.

Preparing wild rice can be tricky. Prepared in the microwave it is much easier and faster. With the addition of currants and nuts you have a perfect make-ahead party dish. As with other grain recipes you can freeze and reheat this wild rice dish.

WILD RICE WITH CURRANTS, MUSHROOMS AND PINE NUTS

1 teaspoon vegetable oil	3/4 cup wild rice
1/4 cup chopped green onion	2 1/2 cups chicken broth
1/2 cup chopped celery	1/2 cup currants
1 cup sliced fresh mushrooms	2 tablespoons pine nuts

1 Combine oil with the green onions, celery and mushrooms in a microsafe bowl. Microcook on High Power 3 minutes or until tender.

2 Rinse rice well, discarding any debris that floats to the surface. Drain. Place wild rice and chicken broth in a 2-quart microsafe casserole. Microcook on High Power 5 minutes, then stir. Microcook on Medium Power (50%) 30 minutes longer. Let stand for 10 minutes, test for doneness and drain off any excess liquid. Fluff with a fork, stir in vegetables, currants and pine nuts.

3 This wild rice dish reheats beautifully. Cover and microcook on High Power until heated through. It also freezes well.

• Serves 4

ORANGE BULGUR PILAF

1/4 cup currants
  2 tablespoons sunflower seeds or slivered almonds
     zest of 1 orange (finely grated orange skin)
3/4 cup orange juice
3/4 cup bulgur or cracked wheat
  1 teaspoon sesame oil
  1 small onion, chopped
1 1/2 cups water

1 In a blender or food processor process currants, sunflower seeds, orange zest and orange juice. Set aside.

2 Place bulgur, sesame oil and onion in a microsafe 2-quart casserole. Microcook on High Power 2 minutes. Stir.

3 In another microsafe container, microcook the water on High Power 5-6 minutes, until boiling. Add water to the bulgur mixture and microcook on High Power 5 minutes.

4 Add the orange mixture and microcook on Medium Power (50%) 12 -14 minutes. Let stand until liquid is absorbed. If it seems too dry add 1/2 cup orange juice and microcook on Medium Power 3 minutes.

• Makes 4 cups (can be frozen)

Since I first tested this recipe I have been making double batches and storing them in zippered plastic bags in our freezer. Unlike the oven or cook top, the microwave is kind to grains when reheating them. This pilaf changes an ordinary meal into a very special one

Here's a fabulous nonfat side dish that you prepare in less than 10 minutes. The ease of preparation, the interesting combination of flavors and unusual presentation make it a perfect 10! In addition to all this, it freezes well. What more can you want?

SAVORY COUSCOUS

1 cup fresh squeezed orange juice
1/2 cup water
1 cup quick cooking couscous
1/2 teaspoon orange zest
   (finely grated orange skin)
1/8 teaspoon ground cardamom

1/8 teaspoon ground ginger
1 teaspoon poppy seed
1/4 teaspoon salt
4 tablespoons nonfat
   plain yogurt or sour cream

Optional Garnish
1 tablespoon chopped pecans
1 teaspoon shredded coconut

1 In a large microsafe casserole, combine the orange juice, water, couscous, orange zest, cardamom, ginger, poppy seeds and salt. Microcook on High Power 5 minutes or until all liquid is absorbed, stirring mid-cycle. Let rest 5 minutes.

2 Stir in yogurt. Garnish with chopped pecans and coconut.

3 Serving portions can be frozen in zippered freezer bags and reheated in the microwave.

Note: If you wish, couscous may be pressed into small ramekins, unmolded on dinner plates and garnished with pecans and coconut for an attractive presentation.

• Serves 4

BARLEY WITH ALMONDS, PEANUTS AND RAISINS

4 cups water	1/4 cup chopped celery
1/2 cup pearl barley	1/8 teaspoon ground cardamom
2 tablespoons raisins	salt
2 tablespoons slivered almonds	& fresh ground pepper to taste
2 tablespoons dry roasted peanuts, chopped	

1   Pour water into a 2-quart microsafe bowl or casserole. Cover and microcook on High Power 8-10 minutes or just until boiling.

2   Add barley to the boiling water and microcook, uncovered, on High Power 30 minutes or until tender. Occasionally stir while cooking.

3   When barley is tender, drain and stir in the raisins, almonds, peanuts, celery, cardamom, salt and pepper.

4   Serve warm as a side dish with roasted or grilled meats.

•   Serves 4

This extremely versatile nonfat barley dish is a 'must fix.' The flavors and texture are unique and it can be served hot or cold. Serve it as a side dish with any meats. Adding a dressing of yogurt, light mayonnaise and lemon juice turns this into a lovely salad. It freezes nicely in a zippered freezer bag and you can take out small servings as you need them. You'd better make a double batch of this recipe.

It's time for you to discover the ease and joy of preparing polenta in the microwave. No constant stirring and no lumps! This tasty version could also serve as a meatless entrée.

CHEESE POLENTA WITH PROVENÇAL SAUCE

Polenta

2 cups water	1/2 teaspoon salt
2/3 cup yellow cornmeal	1/2 cup shredded Mozzarella cheese
1 tablespoon olive oil	& fresh ground pepper

1 Whisk together the water, cornmeal, olive oil and salt in a deep microsafe 3-quart casserole. Cover with lid or plastic wrap and microcook on High Power 6 minutes. Stir once or twice while cooking.

2 Add the Mozzarella cheese and fresh ground pepper to the mixture. Pour into a lightly oiled 8-inch square baking dish. Let stand 3 minutes or until firm.

Sauce

1 tablespoon extra virgin olive oil	1/2 teaspoon fennel seeds
1 small onion, diced	1 (2.2-ounce) can sliced olives
2 cloves garlic, minced	1/4 cup diced sun-dried
1/2 cup canned Italian chopped tomatoes	tomatoes (packed in oil)
1/3 cup minced red bell pepper	2 teaspoons drained capers
1 bay leaf	1 tablespoon minced fresh basil
1/2 teaspoon dried thyme	salt
1 teaspoon orange zest (finely grated orange skin)	& fresh ground pepper

3 To prepare the sauce, combine the oil, onion and garlic in a microsafe bowl. Cover with plastic wrap and microcook on High Power 4 minutes.

4 Stir in the crushed tomatoes, red bell pepper, bay leaf, thyme, orange zest and fennel seeds. Microcook covered on High Power 3 minutes.

5 Stir in the olives, sun-dried tomatoes, capers, salt and pepper to taste.

6 Cut the polenta into four squares and then diagonally into eight triangles. Place on microsafe serving platter or dinner plates and microcook on High Power 1-2 minutes or until heated through.

7 Microcook sauce for 1-3 minutes until very hot. Spoon the sauce over the polenta triangles and top with minced fresh basil. Serve immediately.

- Serves 4

POLENTA WITH RICOTTA AND DRIED FRUIT

Here's another lovely polenta dish. This one is not as firm but has the addition of dried fruit and ricotta cheese. If you like polenta, sometime soon you must try the polenta triangles in the Appetizer chapter.

2 cups water
1 1/2 cups chicken broth
1 cup yellow cornmeal
1/4 teaspoon salt, or to taste
1/2 cup dried cherries or chopped dried apricots
1 1/2 teaspoons lemon zest (finely grated yellow skin)
1 cup ricotta cheese
2 tablespoons butter
3 dashes hot red pepper sauce, or to taste

1 Place the water and chicken broth in a microsafe casserole. Whisk in the cornmeal and salt. Cover with plastic wrap and microcook on High Power 10-12 minutes, or until the liquid is almost completely absorbed. Stir at least three times while cooking.

2 Remove from the oven, add the lemon zest and let stand, covered, 2 minutes.

3 Stir in the ricotta, dried cherries, butter and hot pepper sauce.

4 Reheat in the microwave on High Power 1-3 minutes or until heated through. Serve hot.

• Serves 6

IRISH OATMEAL WITH RAISINS

Oatmeal lovers:
Here's a delightful
breakfast treat.

1 cup water	1/8 teaspoon ground cinnamon
1/4 cup Irish oatmeal	2 tablespoons raisins
1 teaspoon butter	1 tablespoon brown sugar
1/4 teaspoon salt	& warm milk for serving

1 In a 2-quart microsafe bowl combine the water, oatmeal, butter, salt and cinnamon. A large bowl is necessary to keep the oatmeal from boiling over. Microcook covered on High Power 6 minutes, stirring occasionally.

2 Stir in the raisins and microcook covered on High Power 5-7 minutes longer or until almost all the liquid is absorbed.

3 Remove from the oven and let stand covered for 2 minutes. Transfer to a cereal bowl and top with brown sugar and warm milk.

• Serves 1

These nutritious legumes are a taste treat and almost fat free. Italians eat lentils to celebrate the New Year. We can eat these lovely seeds all year for good luck and good health.

LENTILS

1 1/2 pounds green lentils
3 quarts water
3 bay leaves
1 onion stuck with 2 whole cloves
5 garlic cloves, lightly crushed
& salt to taste

1   Place lentils in a large microsafe casserole. Add water to cover by 2 inches, discarding any lentils that rise to the surface and float. Drain well, then return lentils to the casserole and add 3 quarts cold water, plus bay leaves, onion and garlic.

2   Cover with a lid or vented plastic wrap and microcook on High Power 8-10 minutes or until boiling. Stir and microcook on Medium Power (50%) 10 minutes. Add salt and continue to cook on Medium Power for about 10 minutes, until lentils are just tender but not mushy and still hold their shape. If you add the salt too soon it prevents the lentils from softening. The lentils should be firm but not crunchy.

3   Let them cool in the liquid and serve warm or store and use in the following recipe.

•   Serves 12

GRILLED PORTOBELLO MUSHROOMS ON WARM LENTILS WITH MINT VINAIGRETTE

This 4-star restaurant dinner entrée will look lovely, taste terrific and impress your vegetarian friends.

2 cups cooked lentils plus
   a little of their cooking liquid
   (see lentil recipe)
2 garlic cloves, crushed
   salt to taste
& juice of 1/2 lemon

1 tablespoon chopped fresh mint
2 tablespoons olive oil
2 medium portobello mushrooms
   grilled or lightly sautéed with
   olive oil, garlic and lemon juice

1   Microcook lentils in their liquid on High Power 5-8 minutes, or to heat through.

2   Make a paste of the crushed garlic cloves and salt. Combine with the lemon juice, chopped mint and oil.

3   Drain lentils and toss with vinaigrette. Serve right away with slices of grilled portobello mushrooms on the side.

•   Serves 2

MANICOTTI

Manicotti is a marvelous make-ahead casserole. It is enjoyed by all ages, and is quickly cooked in your microwave. In this version of this popular Italian favorite, the manicotti shells are not precooked. This eliminates extra dirty pots to clean and greatly decreases the preparation time. Try using microcooked chicken instead of ground beef for a change of pace!

1 pound lean ground beef
3 (8-ounce) cans tomato sauce
1 cup water
1 tablespoon Italian herb seasoning
1 clove garlic, minced
8 uncooked manicotti shells

12 ounces ricotta cheese
2 tablespoons fresh parsley, minced
1 egg, beaten
1 cup grated Mozzarella cheese
3 tablespoons grated Parmesan cheese

1   To prepare the sauce, crumble ground beef in a large microsafe casserole. Microcook on High Power 4 minutes, stirring twice during cooking. Add tomato sauce, water, Italian herb seasoning and garlic. Pour half the sauce into an 8 x 12-inch microsafe baking dish.

2   Combine the ricotta cheese, parsley, egg, Mozzarella and Parmesan cheese. Spoon this mixture into the uncooked manicotti shells and place them on top of the sauce. Pour remaining sauce over all.

3   Cover with vented plastic wrap and microcook on High Power 5 minutes. Reduce to Medium Power and microcook 25 minutes. Spoon the hot sauce evenly over the manicotti and re-cover with plastic wrap. Let stand 10 minutes. Sprinkle with additional Parmesan cheese before serving.

•   Serves 4

SANDWICHES AND SNACKS

Vegetable Filled Pita Pockets

Pear, Gouda and Chutney Melt

Cheddar, Bacon and Tomato Melt

Tasty Tortilla Melt

Jack Cheese Tortilla with Fresh Tomato Salsa

Diet Watchers' Popcorn Snack

Buttery Caramel Corn

Caramelized Pecans

Chili Cashews

Teriyaki Walnuts

Sugar and Spice Walnuts

Black Bean Burritos

Burrito Pie

SOME MICROWAVE OWNERS firmly believe that the sole use of the microwave is to heat up snacks. Of course, that's only one of the many uses of this unique kitchen helper. In this chapter I've included some unique sandwich and snack ideas as well as new twists on old favorites. Use these basic recipes to create your own sandwiches or snacks.

Popcorn is the ultimate snack! You'll find two great recipes from my popcorn book *Marvelous Microwave Popcorn* (see order blank in back of the book). When microwave manufacturers came out with a popcorn button on their ovens, a whole new industry developed: bagged microwave popcorn. Even though the bags are convenient, they are expensive, contain preservatives our bodies don't need, and can ignite in the microwave. It's better to purchase an inexpensive microwave popcorn popper. With it you use any regular inexpensive popcorn and create healthy, no fat popcorn.

Tortillas and pita bread pockets make wonderful bases for all sorts of snacks. Children have already discovered that fact. The Black Bean Burrito recipe and the Jack Cheese Tortilla with Fresh Tomato Salsa take the tortilla to a higher gastronomic plane.

A number of spiced nut recipes can be found in this chapter. The nuts can be set out in bowls for casual snacking or tossed into salads for a marvelous flavor accent.

Granted, microwave ovens are great for making quick sandwiches and snacks. But you're missing out on a lot of great dining if you stop with those. Why not try one recipe from a different chapter every day this week? Start with a vegetable on Monday, a grain on Tuesday, a chicken recipe on Wednesday and so on during the week. You will be thrilled with the results as you become a more proficient microwave cook. Remember, microwave cooking takes one fourth the time of conventional cooking, doesn't heat up your kitchen, and energy-wise, costs less.

VEGETABLE FILLED PITA POCKETS

Health conscious people will love this vegetable sandwich. Thanks to the microwave, it is very easy to prepare, even for a crowd. Looks quite elegant too.

1/2 cup plain nonfat yogurt	1 cup broccoli florets
1 teaspoon minced fresh dill or 1/2 teaspoon dried dill	1 cup thinly sliced carrots
1 teaspoon minced chives	1 cup thinly sliced mushrooms
1/4 cup chopped cucumbers	4 (6-inch) pita breads
salt	3 green onions, thinly sliced
& pepper	1 cup alfalfa sprouts

1   To prepare yogurt-cucumber dressing: combine yogurt, dill, chives and cucumbers in a small bowl. Season with salt and pepper to taste. Cover and refrigerate.

2   Place the broccoli, sliced carrots and mushrooms in a microsafe bowl and microcook on High Power 5-7 minutes or until vegetables are just tender.

3   Place pita breads between 2 paper towels. Microcook on High Power 1 minute, or until just heated through. Cut each pita in half and fill the pockets with the vegetables. Top with green onions, sprouts and yogurt-cucumber dressing.

•   Serves 4

This recipe has a rather interesting combination of flavors that makes for a most unusual open faced sandwich.

PEAR, GOUDA AND CHUTNEY MELT

1/2 cup grated Gouda cheese (about 2 ounces)
  2 teaspoons minced mango chutney
  1 teaspoon minced fresh parsley
1/2 teaspoon Dijon mustard
  1 slice rye bread, toasted
  4 thin slices ripe pear or tart apple

1 Mix cheese, chutney, parsley and mustard in a small bowl and spread on the rye toast.

2 Place toast on a microsafe dinner plate and microcook on High Power 15-45 seconds, until the cheese melts.

3 Top with pear or apple slices and serve hot.

• Serves 1

CHEDDAR, BACON AND TOMATO MELT

2 slices bacon, halved crosswise
2 slices whole wheat toast
1/2 cup grated Cheddar cheese (about 2 ounces)
1 plum tomato, sliced into 6 thin slices
1 teaspoon minced fresh parsley
& freshly ground black pepper

Here is a new twist to an old favorite. If you are watching fat intake, use a nonfat cheese and eliminate the bacon.

1 Place bacon strips on a bacon cooker or paper towel lined plate. Microcook on High Power 2-3 minutes, until cooked through and crisp.

2 Place toast on a microsafe dinner plate. Sprinkle with half the cheese.

3 Place 2 bacon strips crosswise on top of the cheese. Top with three slices of tomato in a lengthwise pattern.

4 Microcook on High Power 45-90 seconds, just until cheese is melted. Sprinkle with parsley and pepper. Repeat for second sandwich. Serve hot.

• Serves 2

Using jalapeño Jack cheese really adds zip to these easy-to-find ingredients. It makes a quick lunch or fast snack.

TASTY TORTILLA MELT

1 flour tortilla, 7-8 inches in diameter
2 ounces grated jalapeño Monterey Jack cheese
1 thin slice red onion, separated into rings
2 tablespoons corn kernels (fresh, frozen/thawed or canned)
1/4 avocado, peeled, pitted and diced
1 teaspoon minced fresh cilantro
& pinch of crushed hot red pepper flakes

1 Place the tortilla on a microsafe dinner plate. Sprinkle cheese evenly over the top.

2 Scatter the onion rings and corn kernels over the cheese.

3 Microcook on High Power 45-90 seconds, just until cheese is melted.

4 Place the avocado cubes over the melted cheese and season with minced cilantro and hot red pepper flakes. Serve hot.

• Serves 1

JACK CHEESE TORTILLA WITH FRESH TOMATO SALSA

Young people love these tortilla treats. Older people like them too, for lunch or a light dinner.

20 cherry tomatoes, halved
1 ripe medium avocado, peeled, pitted and diced
4 green onions, minced
1 tablespoon fresh lime juice
1 tablespoon minced cilantro
1/4 teaspoon grated lime zest (grated skin of lime)
   salt to taste
1/8 teaspoon ground cumin
1/8 teaspoon cayenne, or to taste
8 flour tortillas (6-inch)
8 ounces Monterey Jack cheese, grated (about 2 cups)
1/2 cup sour cream (optional)

1   To prepare salsa, combine the tomatoes, avocado, green onions, lime juice, cilantro, lime zest, salt, cumin and cayenne in a medium bowl, mixing completely.

2   Place 1 tortilla on a dinner plate and sprinkle with about 1/4 cup grated Monterey Jack cheese. Microcook on High Power 1 minute, or until the cheese is melted.

3   Top with salsa and a dollop of sour cream if you wish. Repeat with the remaining ingredients.

•   Makes 8 tortillas

You won't believe this is diet food when you nibble this wonderful snack.

DIET WATCHERS' POPCORN SNACK

4 cups popped popcorn
8 dried apricot halves, diced
2 tablespoon dark raisins
2 tablespoons golden raisins

1 tablespoon sunflower seeds
1/4 cup light corn syrup
3 tablespoons light brown sugar
1 teaspoon vanilla

1   In a large mixing bowl combine popcorn, apricots, raisins and sunflower seeds. Set aside.

2   In a microsafe bowl combine corn syrup, brown sugar and vanilla. Microcook on High Power until candy thermometer reaches 230°F or until a drop of hot mixture spins a thread when dropped into cold water.

3   Pour hot sugar mixture over popcorn mixture and toss quickly to thoroughly coat.

4   Spray an 8-inch square baking dish with nonstick cooking spray; turn popcorn mixture into pan and using back of spoon, press mixture into pan.

5   Let stand until mixture cools, 5-10 minutes. Invert onto serving dish and cut into four equal portions.

•   Makes 4 (4-inch square) servings

BUTTERY CARAMEL CORN

1	cup brown sugar	1	teaspoon vanilla
1/4	cup light corn syrup	1/2	teaspoon baking soda
1/2	cup margarine	16	cups popped popcorn
1/2	teaspoon salt		

1 Combine sugar, corn syrup, margarine and salt in a large microsafe bowl. Microcook on High Power 2 minutes. Stir well. Continue cooking for 3 minutes, stirring once or twice to help dissolve the sugar. Stir in vanilla and baking soda.

2 Place popcorn in a paper bag (not recycled paper). Pour heated mixture over popcorn and fold bag ends together. Shake well. Keeping the bag closed, microcook on High Power 1 minute (shake bag) microcook 1 minute (shake bag) microcook 30 seconds (shake bag).

3 Pour caramel corn onto a piece of foil and let cool. Store in airtight container.

• Makes 4 quarts

This recipe is taken from my little cookbook 'Marvelous Microwave Popcorn' (see order page at back of this book). You use a paper bag, not for popping the corn, but for mixing the caramel syrup and the popcorn. No clean-up!

CARAMELIZED PECANS

Make your favorite spinach salad, add several fresh strawberries and a few of these yummy pecans and be prepared for compliments. These sugary pecans can also be served as a snack; however, they are addictive so make 2 batches.

2 egg whites
1 cup sugar
20 ounces pecans
2 tablespoons butter

1 Beat egg whites until stiff. Add sugar and nuts. Mix well.

2 Place butter in a large microsafe pie plate and microcook on High Power 30 seconds or until melted.

3 Add coated nuts. Microcook on High Power 9 minutes, stirring twice. Watch carefully as they can burn.

4 Spread on waxed paper to cool. Break apart. Store loosely covered, not in an air-tight container.

• Makes 2-3 cups

CHILI CASHEWS

2 tablespoons butter or margarine
1 1/2 teaspoons chili powder
2 cups salted cashews

1 Place butter in a microsafe bowl. Microcook on High Power
   1 minute or until melted.

2 Stir in chili powder and cashews; coat nuts thoroughly. Microcook
   on High Power 5-7 minutes, stirring twice. Cool. Serve on salads
   or as a snack.

• Makes 2 cups

Here is an interesting, easily prepared snack to have on hand for TV football viewing.

At your next party put out bowls of these spicy nuts and watch them disappear.

TERIYAKI WALNUTS

1/4 cup soy sauce
2 tablespoons sesame oil
1 teaspoon ground ginger
2-3 drops hot pepper sauce
1 tablespoon brown sugar
4 cups walnuts or pecans
(approximately 1 pound)

1 Combine soy sauce, sesame oil, ginger, hot pepper sauce and brown sugar in a 2-quart microsafe casserole. Microcook on High Power 1 minute.

2 Stir in nuts, toss to coat with mixture. Microcook on High Power 3-5 minutes, stirring once or twice, until toasted.

3 Spread evenly on waxed paper to cool. Serve as a snack or topping for salads.

• Makes 4 cups

SUGAR AND SPICE WALNUTS

1/2 cup butter or margarine
3/4 cup brown sugar, packed
   1 teaspoon cinnamon
   4 cups walnuts, approximately 1 pound

1   Place butter in a 1 1/2-quart casserole.

2   Microcook on High Power 1 minute. Stir brown sugar and cinnamon into butter. Microcook on High Power 2 minutes. Mix well to combine.

3   Add the walnuts and mix to coat well. Microcook on High Power 3-5 minutes. Spread on waxed paper to cool. Store in an air-tight container.

•   Makes 4 cups

These sugared walnuts are nice to serve as a holiday treat and also make a great addition to green salads.

Don't let all these ingredients scare you, for this is a wonderful vegetarian snack. The microwave does all the work; you just have to gather up the ingredients.

BLACK BEAN BURRITOS

Bean Burritos

    1 small onion, finely chopped
    2 teaspoons vegetable oil
    1 jalapeño pepper, seeded and diced
    1 clove garlic, minced
  1/4 teaspoon ground cumin
  1/4 teaspoon dried oregano
    1 plum tomato, diced
  1/4 teaspoon ground coriander
  1/4 teaspoon chili powder
    1 (16-ounce) can black beans, drained and rinsed
    3 tablespoons water
    & freshly ground pepper

1   Combine onion, oil, jalapeño pepper and garlic in a microsafe pie plate or bowl. Cover with vented plastic wrap and microcook on High Power 1 minute. Stir in cumin, oregano, coriander and chili powder. Microcook covered 1 minute.

2   Add beans and water to onion mixture and microcook on High Power 2 minutes. Transfer 1/2 cup of the bean mixture to a food processor or blender and purée. Stir back into the remaining beans. Season to taste with salt and pepper.

Salsa

    1/2 ripe avocado, peeled, pitted and diced
      1 green onion, trimmed and minced
      1 tablespoon minced cilantro
      2 teaspoons fresh lime juice
      4 flour tortillas

Optional Garnishes

        shredded romaine lettuce
        diced red onion
        grated Monterey Jack cheese
        sour cream

3 To prepare salsa, combine avocado, tomato, green onion, cilantro and lime juice in a small bowl. Season to taste with salt and pepper.

4 When ready to serve, microcook beans, covered with vented plastic wrap, on High Power 1-3 minutes.

5 To serve, warm 2 tortillas in microwave on High Power 1 minute. Spread with hot beans. Spread salsa and garnishes over each serving. Repeat process for the other two tortillas.

• Serves 2

BURRITO PIE

This unusual Mexican dish is actually layered tortillas with lots of good things in between. Wedges of this pie served with a simple green salad and warmed tortillas make a quick, easy, satisfying meatless dinner.

2 tablespoons butter or margarine
1/4 cup minced onion
1 (17-ounce) can refried beans
1 (3-ounce) package cream cheese
1 (4-ounce) can diced green chiles
1/2 teaspoon garlic salt
1/2 teaspoon bottled Mexican Seasoning (or to taste)

3 (9-inch) flour tortillas
2 cups grated Cheddar cheese
1 (2.2-ounce) can sliced black olives
1/2 cup sour cream
1 tablespoon minced green onion

1 Place butter and minced onion in a microsafe bowl. Microcook on High Power 2-3 minutes, or until onion is soft. Stir in refried beans, cream cheese, chiles, garlic salt and Mexican Seasoning. Cover loosely with waxed paper and microcook on High Power 3 minutes. Stir well to blend in the cream cheese.

2 Place one tortilla on the bottom of a 9-inch quiche dish or pie plate. Top with 1/3 of the bean mixture and 1/3 of the Cheddar cheese. Prepare the pie by repeating this step twice.

3 Cover loosely with waxed paper and microcook on Medium Power (50%) 10-12 minutes or until thoroughly heated. Spread sour cream over top of the pie and sprinkle with the ripe olives and minced green onion. Cut into 6 wedges for serving. Servings can be reheated on High Power 1-2 minutes.

• Makes 6 wedges

SEAFOOD

Fabulous Fish Filets

Lemon Oregano Fish Steaks

Fish Filets Oriental

Cheese Sauced Fish Filets and Asparagus Bundles

Scallop Stuffed Won tons in Basil Butter

Sole with Julienne Vegetables

Sole Florentine

Swordfish Steaks with Parslied Tomatoes and Olives

Salmon Steaks with Avocado Butter

Potatoes Stuffed with Shrimp

Mediterranean Halibut

SEAFOOD IS IDEAL for microwave cooking because of its delicacy and high moisture content.
In addition, microcooking fish requires little or no oil which makes for healthier eating. Seafood microcooks in 5-6 minutes per pound on High Power. Cover most fish with a lid or vented plastic wrap unless it has a crumb coating. However, because of the lack of dry heat in the microwave, a crisp texture can not be obtained.

In this chapter you'll find a variety of seafood dishes. In addition, several of the recipes are 'plate-fixed' dinner recipes. These recipes combine fresh fish, vegetables and seasonings on individual dinner plates which are microcooked just prior to serving.

It's nice to keep a small plastic travel spray bottle filled with lemon juice in your refrigerator. Use it to spritz filets with lemon juice prior to cooking. The lemon juice can also be spritzed on chicken, asparagus spears or broccoli florets prior to cooking, to enhance their delicate flavors. A little spray bottle of lemon juice is also a great boon to health conscious eaters.

You really must try fish in the microwave. You won't believe how moist and flavorful it can be.

FABULOUS FISH FILETS

2 fish filets (6-8 ounces each)
1/2 cup nonfat yogurt or sour cream
1 tablespoon chopped fresh dill,
   or 1 teaspoon dried dill
1/4 cup Parmesan cheese

1 Place filets in a microsafe baking dish. Spread yogurt or sour cream over filets. Sprinkle with dill and Parmesan cheese.

2 Cover with vented plastic wrap and microcook on High Power 5-6 minutes per pound. Fish is ready to serve when it flakes easily when pierced with a fork.

• Serves 2

Healthy eating is important to all of us. These filets are good for us and taste great!

LEMON OREGANO FISH STEAKS

This fresh herb marinade adds marvelous flavors to fish steaks. They look lovely on a dinner plate when garnished with fresh oregano sprigs and lemon wedges.

2 tablespoons olive oil
2 tablespoons fresh lemon juice
2 strips lemon peel, cut into fine julienne
1 teaspoon chopped fresh oregano leaves,
   (or 1/4 teaspoon dried oregano)
1 clove garlic, crushed
2 (1-inch thick) swordfish, red snapper
   or other fish steaks (about 8 ounces each)
   freshly ground pepper
   fresh oregano sprigs for garnish
& lemon wedges for garnish

1 Combine olive oil, lemon juice, lemon peel, oregano and garlic in a microsafe pie plate. Add fish steaks and turn to coat with the marinade. Marinate at room temperature at least 30 minutes (or refrigerate and marinate up to 1 hour).

2 Cover pie plate with vented plastic wrap and microcook on High Power 4-5 minutes, or until just cooked through.

3 Spoon marinade over the steaks; sprinkle generously with pepper and garnish with fresh oregano sprigs and lemon wedges.

• Serves 2

FISH FILETS ORIENTAL

This oriental
treatment for fish is
a nice flavor change.

1 1/2 teaspoons sesame seeds	1 teaspoon soy sauce
2 (6-8 ounce) flounder, sole	1 clove garlic, crushed
or orange roughy filets	2 green onions, trimmed
1 tablespoon sesame oil	and cut into thin diagonal slices
2 teaspoons grated fresh ginger	(for garnish)

1   Sprinkle the sesame seeds on a microsafe plate. Microcook on High Power 1-2 minutes until lightly toasted. Set aside.

2   Arrange the fish filets in a single layer on a microsafe dinner plate.

3   In a small bowl combine the sesame oil, ginger, soy sauce and garlic. Spread this mixture evenly over the surface of the filets.

4   Cover with vented plastic wrap. Microcook on High Power 2 minutes. Turn the plate 180° and cook 1-2 minutes, or until fish flakes slightly.

5   Place filets on dinner plates and sprinkle with toasted sesame seeds and green onions.

•   Serves 2

Here is another colorful, complete dinner in one easy recipe. You will be amazed when you discover how quickly and perfectly your microwave cooks these fish bundles and the wine-cheese sauce that tops them.

CHEESE SAUCED FISH FILETS AND ASPARAGUS BUNDLES

Bundles
  10 ounces fresh asparagus
   4 sole, flounder or orange roughy filets
     (4 ounces each)

1 Place filets on a flat surface, boned side down. Place 1/4 of the asparagus spears across the narrow end of each filet.

2 Starting at the narrow end, roll up each fish filet around the spears.

3 Place fish-asparagus bundles in a microsafe baking dish, seam side down. Cover with vented plastic wrap and microcook on High Power 4-6 minutes or until fish flakes easily when tested with a fork.

4 Place bundles on a platter; keep warm.

Cheese Sauce

   1 tablespoon butter or margarine
1/2 cup milk
   2 tablespoons white wine
   1 tablespoon flour
1/2 teaspoon salt
1/8 teaspoon ground red pepper
1/2 cup grated Cheddar cheese
   4 lemon slices for garnish

5 Into the cooking liquid in baking dish, add the butter; whisk in the milk, wine, flour, salt and pepper. Microcook on High Power 3-4 minutes, until sauce thickens slightly, stirring twice.

6 Stir cheese into sauce. Microcook on High Power 1 minute; stir until smooth. Spoon over bundles and garnish with lemon slices if you wish.

- Serves 4

This sounds pretty fancy but it truly is very simple to prepare and is quite impressive when served on individual plates as an appetizer or a light entrée.

SCALLOP STUFFED WON TONS IN BASIL BUTTER

Scallop-Mushroom Mixture

1 tablespoon butter or margarine	1/8 teaspoon pepper
1 green onion, sliced	1/4 teaspoon salt
1 tablespoon flour	8 ounces fresh mushrooms,
8 ounces sea scallops	chopped

1   In a 1-quart microsafe casserole combine 1 tablespoon butter and the green onion. Microcook on High Power 1 minute. Stir in the flour to form a paste.

2   Chop scallops using steel blade of processor or chopping knife, reserve. Add mushrooms, scallops, salt and pepper to flour mixture. Stir to mix well. Microcook on High Power 6 minutes to form a moist paste. Stir halfway through cooking.

Won ton Preparation

4 quarts water
1 tablespoon water
1 teaspoon cornstarch
48 won ton skins

3   Bring the 4 quarts of water to a boil in a stockpot on top of the stove.

4   In a small bowl combine the cornstarch with 1 tablespoon water until smooth.

5 Place a heaping teaspoon of scallop mixture in the center of a won ton skin. Brush edges of the skin with the cornstarch mixture. Fold in half with points touching, to form a triangle. Repeat with the other skins.

6 When water boils, drop in 16 filled won tons. Boil for 5-6 minutes, Remove with a slotted spoon and repeat with remaining won tons. Keep warm.

Basil Butter

   8 tablespoons butter
1/4 cup chopped fresh basil
     freshly grated Parmesan cheese
  & whole basil leaves for garnish

7 In a medium size microsafe bowl, combine the remaining 8 tablespoons butter and the chopped basil. Microcook on High Power 1-2 minutes or until the butter is melted.

8 Arrange 3-5 cooked won tons on each plate. Spoon the basil butter on top and sprinkle generously with Parmesan cheese. Garnish each plate with a basil leaf.

• Serves 6-8

Colorful julienne vegetables peeking out of rolled sole filets make this not only healthy, but a beautiful entrée presentation as well. Another elegant plate-fixed dinner.

SOLE WITH JULIENNE VEGETABLES

2 ounces unpeeled zucchini, cut into julienne
1 small carrot, peeled and cut into julienne
1/2 red pepper, cut into julienne
1/2 teaspoon soy sauce
1 teaspoon sesame oil

2 pieces filet of sole or orange roughy (6 ounces each)
2 teaspoons fresh lemon juice
salt
freshly ground pepper
2 thin slices lemon

1   Combine zucchini, carrots and red pepper with soy sauce in a microsafe glass casserole. Cover and microcook on High Power 1-2 minutes or until crisp-tender. Pour off the liquid. Add the sesame oil, toss to coat and set aside.

2   Place the sesame seeds on a microsafe dinner plate and microcook on High Power 6 minutes, stirring every 2 minutes, until the seeds are lightly toasted.

3   Place the fish filets in a microsafe pie plate; sprinkle with lemon juice, a pinch of salt and some freshly ground pepper.

4   Divide the vegetables between the pieces of filet, fold the filets tip to tip over the vegetables, pulling strips out of each end for a decorative touch. Top each folded filet with a lemon slice. Cover loosely with waxed paper and microcook on High Power 2 minutes. Turn the plate 180° and microcook 2 minutes longer. Let stand covered 1 minute.

Garnish

1 1/2 tablespoons sesame seeds
 1/4 cup chopped fresh parsley

5 Sprinkle filets with toasted sesame seeds and chopped parsley. You might sprinkle a little of the chopped parsley around the rim of the plate for an even more colorful presentation.

• Serves 2

SOLE FLORENTINE

Another delicious 'dinner in a dish' but this one is also low in fat and in calories!

2 (10-ounce) packages frozen, chopped spinach
8 medium, sliced mushrooms,
2 tablespoons dehydrated, chopped onion
1/2 teaspoon lemon zest (grated yellow skin)
1/2 teaspoon salt
1/2 teaspoon fresh ground pepper
1/2 teaspoon dry mustard
2 tablespoons grated Parmesan cheese
2 teaspoons chopped fresh parsley
1/2 teaspoon paprika
1 pound sole filets

1 Pierce frozen spinach packages and place them in the microwave oven. Microcook on High Power 6-7 minutes, or until packages flex easily. Drain spinach well, squeezing out all liquid.

2 Place drained spinach in a microsafe baking dish. Stir in mushroom slices, onion, lemon zest, salt, pepper and dry mustard. Spread spinach mixture evenly over bottom of baking dish.

3 Combine Parmesan cheese, parsley and paprika. Set aside.

4 Place fish on top of the spinach mixture. Cover loosely with waxed paper and microcook on High Power 4 minutes. Rearrange fish pieces and sprinkle with Parmesan mixture. Cover with waxed paper and microcook on High Power 2-4 minutes or until fish flakes easily.

• Serves 4

SWORDFISH STEAKS
WITH PARSLIED TOMATOES AND OLIVES

Another colorful, healthy dinner entrée. Microwaves and fish were meant for each other!

  2 swordfish steaks, about 8 ounces each
  1 (16-ounce) can whole tomatoes, drained and sliced
1/4 cup chopped fresh parsley
1/3 cup chopped pitted black olives
  1 tablespoon olive oil
  1 tablespoon lemon juice
   salt
& pepper

1 Place sliced tomatoes on a microsafe pie plate. Sprinkle the parsley and black olives over the layer of tomatoes.

2 Place swordfish steaks over the parslied tomatoes and drizzle with olive oil and lemon juice. Sprinkle lightly with salt and pepper.

3 Cover plate with plastic wrap and microcook on High Power 5 minutes. Remove from the oven, puncture plastic wrap and let sit 2 minutes.

4 Place steaks on dinner plates and spoon sauce over.

• Serves 2

SALMON STEAKS WITH AVOCADO BUTTER

These nicely flavored seafood steaks are enhanced by a sharply seasoned avocado butter. The avocado butter can also be served on grilled or pan fried fish steaks.

2 tablespoons water
2 tablespoons white wine vinegar
1 tablespoon lemon juice
1/4 teaspoon paprika
1/4 teaspoon ground cumin
    dash liquid smoke
1/4 teaspoon salt
1/8 teaspoon white pepper
6 salmon steaks
    (about 2 1/2 pounds, each steak 1/2 to 3/4-inch thick)
    Halibut or swordfish may be substituted for the salmon
& cilantro or parsley sprigs for garnish

1 Combine water, vinegar, lemon juice, paprika, cumin, liquid smoke, salt and pepper in an 8 x 12-inch microsafe baking dish. Place fish steaks in baking dish, turning over to coat with vinaigrette. Let stand 20 minutes.

2 Prepare the Avocado Butter (see next page)

3 Microcook the salmon, covered with vented plastic wrap, on High Power 4-5 minutes per pound or until fish is tender and flakes with a fork. Rotate baking dish after 4 minutes. Arrange salmon steaks on a serving platter or individual plates. Garnish with cilantro or parsley and serve with Avocado Butter.

Avocado Butter

      3 large sprigs parsley
    1/2 clove garlic
      4 ounces butter or margarine, softened
      1 large ripe avocado, peeled, pitted, cut into 1-inch pieces
      3 teaspoons lime juice
    1/4 teaspoon chili powder
    1/8 teaspoon cayenne pepper

1 In processor bowl fitted with steel knife, process parsley until minced. With machine running, drop garlic through feed tube; process until minced.

2 Add butter, avocado, lime juice, chili powder and cayenne pepper. Process until smooth, scraping sides of bowl with spatula when necessary.

3 Refrigerate in a covered container, or freeze for later use.

• Serves 6

POTATOES STUFFED WITH SHRIMP

If you use nonfat milk and nonfat cheese you'll have a healthier dinner. For a simple supper, prepare this ahead of time and just reheat for a few minutes. While your microwave heats the entrée, you can toss a green salad and dinner is ready.

2 large baking potatoes
(about 6 ounces each)
8 ounces shelled and
deveined shrimp,
coarsely chopped
1 tablespoon olive oil
1/2 clove garlic, crushed
1/8 teaspoon dried thyme

1/4 cup milk or half and half
1/2 cup coarsely grated
Cheddar cheese
(about 2 ounces)
2 tablespoons minced chives
or green part of green onion
salt
& freshly ground pepper

1 With a tip of a paring knife, pierce the scrubbed potatoes at least twice. Microcook on High Power 7-9 minutes or until the potatoes feel almost tender when pierced with a knife tip. Wrap in foil and let stand until ready to serve.

2 Combine the shrimp, olive oil, garlic and thyme in a microsafe shallow bowl. Stir to blend. Cover with plastic wrap and microcook 2 minutes. Uncover, stir well, re-cover and let stand 1 minute.

3 Cut a thin slice from the top of each cooked potato. Using a teaspoon, scoop out the cooked potato, leaving a firm shell. Reserve the shells.

4 In a large bowl, mash the cooked potato. Add the cooked shrimp, milk, half of the cheese and half of the chives. Stir until well blended. Add salt and pepper to taste.

5 Spoon back into the reserved potato shells and sprinkle with the remaining 1/4 cup cheese, dividing evenly.

6 Place on a microsafe dinner plate and microcook on High Power 1 minute, or until the cheese is melted. Sprinkle with the remaining 1 tablespoon chives.

7 If you're preparing this to serve later, you can stuff the potato shells and just prior to serving, microcook them on High Power 5-8 minutes or until heated through. Then top with cheese and microcook 1 minute or until cheese is melted.

• Serves 2

These fish filets look beautiful on a plate and the red peppers, olives and capers add a surprisingly nice flavor.

MEDITERRANEAN HALIBUT

1 pound halibut or other lean fish filets
2 tablespoons lemon juice
1 tablespoon chopped onion, or 1/2 tablespoon dried onion
2 tablespoons chopped red pepper
1 tablespoon coarsely chopped pimiento-stuffed olives
1 tablespoon capers
1 tablespoon olive oil

1 Cut filets into 4 serving pieces. Arrange fish, thickest parts to outside edges, in an 8 x 8-inch square microsafe dish.

2 Mix lemon juice, chopped onion, red peppers, olives, capers and oil together and spread over fish.

3 Cover and refrigerate at least 30 minutes, but no longer than 6 hours.

4 Cover with vented plastic wrap and microcook on High Power 3 minutes; rotate dish and microcook 3-5 minutes longer, or until fish flakes easily with a fork. Let stand covered 3 minutes.

• Serves 4

POULTRY

Chicken, Tomatoes, Basil and Goat Cheese in Parchment

Chicken Breasts with Fresh Tomato Salsa

Spicy Ginger Almond Chicken

Oriental Chicken with Vegetables and Soba Noodles

Ginger Chicken Breasts and Vegetables in Parchment

Cantonese Chicken

Chicken Breasts with Water Chestnuts, Lemon and Ginger

Chicken Cacciatore

Company Chicken

Peppered Citrus Chicken Breasts

Raspberry Sauced Turkey Tenderloins

Turkey Cutlets with Sun-dried Tomatoes, Herbs and Cheese

Chicken Breasts with Roasted Red Pepper Purée

Smoked Chicken

Chicken with Corn Salsa

POULTRY COOKS TO PERFECTION in the microwave.
To reduce the fat and cholesterol substantially, remove the skin before cooking. Since microwave cooking retains moisture, the poultry won't dry out as it would in a conventional oven.

Lots of talk these days about sanitizing wooden cutting boards and sponges after cutting up chicken. Dan Cliver, a microbiologist at the University of Wisconsin states that you can microcook kitchen sponges (1 minute) and wooden cutting boards (5 minutes) on High Power to rid them of bacteria. Plastic cutting boards go into the dishwasher for sanitizing.

Poultry combines well with vegetables and a variety of sauces. It may be served alone or with rice, pasta or potatoes. A simple trick is to prepare double batches of one of the grain recipes, freeze in plastic zipper bags and later take out as much as you need, reheat on High Power to serving temperature and combine with a poultry recipe for a marvelous, quick dinner.

Poaching boneless chicken or turkey cutlets provides readily cooked morsels for use in salads, sandwiches or casseroles. To poach a boneless chicken breast, place one-half chicken breast on a microsafe plate, season with 1 teaspoon lemon juice or white wine, salt and pepper, and cover with vented plastic wrap. Microcook on High Power 3-4 minutes. For larger portions, prepare in same manner, placing meatier sections on the outside of the plate and microcook on High Power 6-7 minutes per pound.

In this chapter you will find two unusual turkey cutlet recipes, many chicken recipes and a 'plate-fixed' chicken and salsa recipe. These 'plate-fixed' dinners (see index) are a great boon to busy people. Simply combine the fresh ingredients on a dinner plate, cover with vented plastic wrap and refrigerate until 3 minutes before serving time. Microcook each plate on High Power 3-4 minutes and dinner is ready. It's just that simple!

CHICKEN, TOMATOES, BASIL AND GOAT CHEESE IN PARCHMENT

4 large tomato slices
4 teaspoons shredded fresh basil or 1/2 teaspoon dried
3 ounces mild goat cheese cut into 8 thin rounds
2 skinless, boneless chicken breast halves
1 large garlic clove, minced
& parchment paper

1   Cut off two 14-inch sheets of parchment. Place 1 tomato slice on each piece of parchment. Sprinkle basil over the tomato slices and place 2 cheese rounds on top of the basil. Place 1 chicken breast half on top of this first tomato, cheese and basil layer. Then add 1 tomato slice, garlic, remaining basil and 2 cheese rounds on top of each chicken breast.

2   Gather up the four corners of parchment with both hands and twist into a bundle to enclose the chicken or fold the bundles into square packages. Repeat with second chicken breast package. Place both bundles on a dinner plate. Microcook on High Power 5-6 minutes. Let stand 2 minutes before serving.

•   Serves 2

This recipe will soon be your favorite 'Quick Fix' dinner entrée. What makes it great? It is low in calories and is quickly prepared. To make it more festive for company, tie a ribbon or kitchen twine around each twisted parchment bundle before cooking. Add a serving of Savory Couscous (from the Grain chapter) and a green salad; dinner guests will praise your cooking prowess.

CHICKEN BREASTS WITH FRESH TOMATO SALSA

Here is another 'Quick Fix' dinner. It's colorful, low in fat, very quickly prepared and tastes divine. You might serve this entrée with a green salad and warm flour tortillas, Mexican beer or seltzer with a squeeze of lime. You can easily halve or double the recipe.

1/2 cup avocado, peeled, seeded and diced
4 cherry tomatoes, quartered
1 green onion, minced
1/2 jalapeño pepper, seeded and minced
1 tablespoon minced cilantro
1/4 teaspoon fresh lime juice, or to taste

1/2 teaspoon ground cumin
1/8 teaspoon chili powder or to taste
1/8 teaspoon salt
2 boneless and skinless chicken breast halves
1 tablespoon white wine or lemon juice

1 Combine the avocado, cherry tomatoes, green onion, jalapeño pepper, cilantro, lime juice, ground cumin, chili powder and salt in a small bowl. Set aside at room temperature.

2 Place the chicken breast halves on a microsafe dinner plate, with thicker portions toward the outside of the plate. Drizzle with the wine or lemon juice. Cover with vented plastic wrap and microcook on High Power 3-4 minutes, turning plate after 2 minutes. Let stand covered until ready to serve.

3 Add the juices from the cooked chicken to the salsa. Place the warm chicken on plates and top with the salsa. Serve immediately.

• Serves 2

SPICY GINGER ALMOND CHICKEN

These spicy coated chicken breasts are a refreshing treat. They are simple to prepare and ready in just minutes.

1 1/4 cup almonds
3/4 cup orange marmalade
1/4 cup soy sauce
1 tablespoon Dijon mustard
2 teaspoons grated fresh ginger
1 clove garlic, minced
1/2 teaspoon curry powder
1/4 teaspoon red pepper flakes
8 chicken breast halves, skinned and boned

1   Finely chop almonds in a food processor. Spread on a microsafe plate and microcook on High Power 2 minutes or until lightly toasted, stirring after first minute to avoid burning.

2   Combine almonds with the marmalade, soy sauce, mustard, ginger, garlic, curry powder and red pepper flakes.

3   Coat the chicken with the almond mixture. Place breasts in a microsafe casserole. Cover with vented plastic wrap and microcook 10-12 minutes. Serve warm or cold.

•   Serves 6-8

Here is another low fat chicken and vegetable dinner for you to serve your family.

ORIENTAL CHICKEN WITH VEGETABLES AND SOBA NOODLES

4 boneless skinless chicken breasts
   (3 or 4 ounce)
1 teaspoon grated fresh ginger
1/4 teaspoon minced garlic
2 tablespoons soy sauce
1 tablespoon orange juice
1 teaspoon rice vinegar
8 large red radishes, thinly sliced

8 large mushrooms,
   thinly sliced
4 green onions, cut into
   1/2-inch pieces
6 broccoli florets, thinly sliced
4 ounces soba noodles
   or angel hair pasta

1 Place the chicken breasts in a large microsafe casserole. Combine the ginger, garlic, soy sauce, orange juice and rice vinegar together and spread over each chicken breast.

2 Sprinkle the radishes, mushrooms, green onions and broccoli over the 4 sauced chicken breasts. Cover with vented plastic wrap and microcook on High Power 6-8 minutes or until chicken is cooked through and the vegetables are crisp-tender.

3 Cook the soba noodles or pasta in the conventional way and drain. Place on 4 dinner plates. Spoon the vegetables and chicken over each serving.

• Serves 4

GINGER CHICKEN BREASTS AND VEGETABLES IN PARCHMENT

2 bok choy stalks	1/2 small onion, chopped
1 small red bell pepper, cut into thin strips	16 snow peas, trimmed
	2 skinless boneless chicken breast halves
4 large mushrooms, thinly sliced	2 teaspoons minced fresh ginger
	2 teaspoons soy sauce

1 Remove and reserve green leaves from bok choy. Cut white part of bok choy stalks into thin strips.

2 Cut two 10 x 14-inch pieces of parchment. Place 1 bok choy leaf on each.

3 Combine the pepper strips, mushrooms, onions and snow peas. Arrange 1/4 of the vegetables on each leaf. Place chicken on top of vegetables. Sprinkle 1 teaspoon minced ginger and 1 teaspoon soy sauce over each. Top with remaining vegetables.

4 Gather up the 4 corners of parchment square and twist into a bundle or fold into a package. (You may tie each bundle with twine or ribbon if you wish). Microcook on High Power 5-6 minutes. Let stand 2 minutes before serving.

• Serves 2

Foods wrapped in parchment cook beautifully in the microwave. The soy sauce and fresh ginger in this recipe gently flavor the fresh vegetables and chicken.

This recipe is a low fat microwave stir fry. Serve it over hot rice (cooked in the microwave, of course).

CANTONESE CHICKEN

12 ounces skinless, boneless chicken breast halves (3-4)
 1 cup broccoli florets
 1 cup cauliflower florets
1/2 pound mushrooms, sliced
 4 green onions, cut into 1-inch pieces
 2 tablespoons low sodium soy sauce
 3 tablespoon dry sherry
 1 teaspoon grated fresh ginger
 1 teaspoon arrowroot dissolved in 2 tablespoons water
 1 teaspoon sesame oil
1/4 cup unsalted peanuts, coarsely chopped

1 Slice chicken breasts into thin strips. Arrange slices in a microsafe rectangular casserole. Cover with waxed paper and microcook on High Power 6-7 minutes, turning occasionally, until cooked through. Wrap in foil and set aside.

2 Combine broccoli, cauliflower, mushrooms, onions, soy sauce, sherry and ginger in a microsafe bowl. Microcook on High Power 6-8 minutes, stirring occasionally.

3 Add dissolved arrowroot, sesame oil, peanuts and chicken pieces. Stir to combine, and microcook on High Power 2 minutes or until warmed through.

• Serves 4

CHICKEN BREASTS WITH WATER CHESTNUTS, LEMON AND GINGER

2 skinless boneless chicken breast halves
1/4 cup minced green onion
2 tablespoons soy sauce
2 teaspoons lemon juice
2 teaspoons minced fresh ginger
1 clove garlic, minced
10 canned water chestnuts, coarsely chopped
& fresh ground pepper

1 Place chicken in a shallow microsafe baking dish. Sprinkle onion over chicken.

2 Combine soy sauce, lemon juice, ginger, garlic, water chestnuts and pepper. Pour mixture over the chicken.

3 Cover loosely with waxed paper. Microcook on High Power 5-7 minutes.

• Serves 2

This appealing no fat chicken recipe has an unusual combination of ingredients. The crunch of water chestnuts combined with lemon and ginger for flavor produce a healthy, savory entrée.

CHICKEN CACCIATORE

A fellow participant in a writing class gave me this marvelous microwave recipe. It's an easily prepared dish to serve to a crowd.

3 pounds chicken parts
or boneless skinless chicken breasts
1 (15-ounce) can tomato sauce
1 (6-ounce) can tomato paste
1 cup water
1/2 cup dry red wine
1/2 cup dehydrated,
chopped onions

1 (2.2-ounce) can pitted,
sliced, ripe olives
1/2 cup sliced fresh mushrooms
3 cloves garlic, minced
1 tablespoon dried oregano
1/2 teaspoon salt
1/2 teaspoon dried thyme
1 teaspoon dried basil

1 Combine the tomato sauce, tomato paste, water, wine, onions, olives, mushrooms, garlic, oregano, salt, thyme and basil in a 4-quart microsafe casserole. Stir to blend.

2 Add the chicken pieces. Cover with a lid or vented plastic wrap. Microcook on High Power 10 minutes. Stir and continue cooking on High Power 15 minutes, rotating the dish occasionally.

Note: You might serve this over hot buttered noodles sprinkled with poppy seeds. This can be frozen, so make a big batch. You'll be glad you did.

• Serves 10

COMPANY CHICKEN

3 1/2 ounces canned french fried onions, crushed
  1/4 cup bread crumbs
    2 teaspoons paprika
       salt
    4 tablespoons sour cream
    6 boneless, skinless chicken breast halves

1 Combine crushed french fried onions, bread crumbs, paprika and salt in a shallow bowl.

2 Place sour cream in another shallow bowl. Dip chicken pieces in sour cream to coat; then in crumb and herb mixture.

3 Place coated chicken pieces, in a circle, on a microsafe plate. Do not cover. Cook on High Power 10-12 minutes.

• Serves 6

My good friend Alberta likes to serve this to company. It is delicious and so easy to prepare ahead of time. Serve your guests salad while the chicken cooks!

Don't skimp on the lemon pepper in this recipe, as it really adds interesting flavor to this low fat chicken entrée.

PEPPERED CITRUS CHICKEN BREASTS

4 (3 or 4 ounce) skinless,
   boneless chicken breast halves
1 tablespoon grated Parmesan cheese
1 tablespoon chopped fresh parsley
2 teaspoons orange zest
   (grated orange skin only)

1/4 cup orange juice
1 tablespoon white wine
1 teaspoon lemon juice
2 medium oranges,
   peeled and segmented
2 teaspoons lemon pepper

1 Place the chicken breasts around the outer rim of a microsafe pie plate.

2 Combine the Parmesan cheese, parsley, orange zest, orange juice, wine and lemon juice. Pour over the chicken. Cover with vented plastic wrap and microcook on High Power 4 minutes.

3 Turn the breasts over, add the orange segments to the center of the plate. Cover again and microcook on High Power for 4-6 minutes or until the chicken is cooked. Let stand for 3 minutes.

4 To serve, slice each chicken breast into 4 pieces and divide the pieces among 4 dinner plates. Surround the chicken with the orange segments. Spoon the cooking juices over the chicken and sprinkle each serving with 1/2 teaspoon lemon pepper.

• Serves 4

RASPBERRY SAUCED TURKEY TENDERLOINS

Turkey is such a
wonderful low fat
tasty protein source.
Here is a flavorful
healthy entrée for
family or friends.

1/2 cup seedless raspberry jam
  6 tablespoons raspberry vinegar
  4 tablespoons Dijon mustard
  2 teaspoons orange zest (grated orange skin)
1/2 teaspoon dried basil
    salt
    freshly ground pepper to taste
  4 turkey breast tenderloins, about 6 ounces each

1 Place raspberry jam, vinegar, mustard, orange zest and basil in a 3-quart microsafe baking dish. Stir until well blended.

2 Place turkey tenderloins in sauce and turn to coat well. Cover with vented plastic wrap and microcook on High Power 4-5 minutes.

3 Brush tenderloins with sauce and rearrange with uncooked portions toward outside of dish. Microcook, uncovered, on High Power 6-7 minutes, or until meat is no longer pink in thickest part; cut to test.

4 Season to taste with salt and pepper.

• Serves 4

Here is another busy day recipe you can prepare ahead of time and then pop in the microwave for 6-9 minutes. The colorful slices look smashing on a dinner plate. A green salad and French bread is all you need to complete this elegant dinner for 4.

TURKEY CUTLETS WITH SUN-DRIED TOMATOES, HERBS AND CHEESE

4 large pieces sun-dried tomatoes in oil, finely chopped
1 (4-ounce) package soft garlic and herb cheese
1/4 cup shredded Mozzarella cheese
1 teaspoon fresh chopped rosemary
5 basil leaves, chopped
4 turkey cutlets (3 to 4 ounces each)
2 tablespoons butter or margarine
1/2 cup seasoned dried bread crumbs
   salt
& freshly ground pepper

1 In a bowl, combine herb cheese, Mozzarella, rosemary, basil and sun-dried tomatoes.

2 Spoon an equal amount of filling onto 1 end of each cutlet and roll up jelly roll fashion. Secure with wooden toothpicks.

3 Place butter in a microsafe bowl and Microcook on High Power 45 seconds or until melted.

4 Place bread crumbs on a large piece of waxed paper and sprinkle with salt and pepper.

5 Dip turkey rolls in melted butter, then coat in bread crumbs. Rolls may be refrigerated until ready to cook.

6 Arrange the 4 rolls, end to end in a circle, on the outer edge of a large microsafe plate. Cover loosely with waxed paper and microcook on High Power 6-9 minutes or until fork-tender. Let stand a few minutes before slicing.

7 To serve, cut into 1/2-inch slices and arrange overlapping slices on individual dinner plates.

• Serves 4

Here is another low fat healthy chicken entrée. Placing the sliced chicken breast atop this unusual sauce will rival fancy restaurant fare.

CHICKEN BREASTS WITH ROASTED RED PEPPER PURÉE

Chicken

    1 tablespoon olive oil
  1/2 clove garlic, crushed
    1 teaspoon minced fresh oregano leaves,
        or 1/2 teaspoon dried oregano
    4 boneless, skinless chicken breast halves

1 Combine the oil, garlic and oregano on a plate. Coat the chicken breasts with the oil mixture and arrange in a microsafe pie plate. Cover with vented plastic wrap and microcook on High Power 6-8 minutes. Turn over the breasts and check to see that they are cooked through or no longer pink. Pour broth into bowl of food processor fitted with the steel blade. Place chicken breasts on a plate, cover and let stand while preparing the sauce.

Roasted Red Pepper Purée

    1 tablespoon olive oil
  1/4 cup minced onion
    1 (7-ounce) jar roasted red peppers, rinsed and drained
    2 tablespoons finely chopped fresh parsley

2 Combine the olive oil and onion in a microsafe bowl and microcook on High Power 3 minutes, or until the onion is tender.

3 Add the drained peppers to the broth in the processor and process briefly. Add the cooked onion to the pepper purée and process until smooth. Taste for seasoning. Microcook on High Power 2-3 minutes or until serving temperature.

4 Cut the cooked chicken breasts into 1/4-inch thick diagonal slices. Spoon the sauce onto the center of four dinner plates, dividing evenly. Arrange the chicken slices slightly overlapping over the sauce and sprinkle with chopped parsley.

● Serves 4

If you would like some smoked chicken to toss in a green salad or for a sandwich, this is an easy no-hassle recipe. Smoked chicken in the microwave? Try it you'll like it!

SMOKED CHICKEN

1/4 cup soy sauce
1/3 cup liquid smoke
  3 boneless skinless chicken breast halves

1   Combine soy sauce and liquid smoke, add chicken breasts and marinate for 6-8 hours.

2   Place chicken breasts on a microsafe plate, cover with vented plastic wrap and microcook on High Power 8-9 minutes.

•   Makes 2-3 cups chopped or slivered smoked chicken

CHICKEN WITH CORN SALSA

1/2 cup canned whole kernel corn
1/2 cup diced ripe tomato
  2 tablespoons diced red bell pepper
  2 tablespoons diced green bell pepper
  2 tablespoons chopped cilantro
  2 tablespoons red wine vinegar
  2 tablespoons olive oil
  1 clove garlic, minced
1/2 teaspoon ground cumin
1/4 teaspoon salt
     freshly ground black pepper
     pinch of cayenne pepper
  2 boneless chicken breast halves (about 5 ounces each)
     salt
     pepper
  & fresh cilantro sprigs (for garnish)

1 Combine corn kernels, diced tomato, red bell pepper, green bell pepper, cilantro, red wine vinegar, olive oil, garlic and cumin in a small bowl.

2 Flatten each chicken breast with a meat mallet, to a thickness of 1/4-inch. Cut each half-breast into four long strips. Lightly season them with salt and pepper.

3 Divide the salsa and spread over the entire surface of two microsafe dinner plates.

Here is a 'Quick Fix' dinner cooked on a plate. When you have a busy day ahead of you, prepare this delectable dinner in the morning and refrigerate. At dinner time, pop each plate in the microwave for 3 minutes and out comes this colorful healthy dinner. Try it. I am certain you'll like it!

4 Arrange four strips of chicken around the edge of each plate, forming a large square.

5 Cover each plate with vented plastic wrap. Microcook each portion separately on High Power 3 minutes. Garnish with a sprig of cilantro and serve immediately.

- Serves 2

MEAT

Pork Chops Gruyère

Roast Pork Loin with Sweet Potato Stuffing

Fresh Herb Stuffed Pork Loin with Mustard Sauce

Ginger Beef and Vegetable Bundles

Teriyaki Beef Kabobs

Beef Stuffed Bell Peppers

Fast Fix Pot Roast

South of the Border Casserole

Honey Mustard Glazed Corned Beef

Spaghetti Squash with Ham and Peppers

Sausage Potato Brunch Dish

Dinner in a Potato

MANY PEOPLE BELIEVE that red meat can't be cooked in the microwave. This is not true, as evidenced by the recipes in this chapter. You will find recipes for large cuts of meat, chops and ground beef. There are times when you'll want to barbecue, broil or pan fry your meat. However, I do urge you to try some of these fast and easy microwave meat recipes. You'll be pleasantly surprised and pleased with Pork Chops Gruyére, Honey Mustard Glazed Corned Beef, Fast Fix Pot Roast and South of the Border Casserole.

On extra busy days look in the index under 'plate-fixed' dinners. The meat, vegetables and seasonings in these recipes are literally placed on a dinner plate, covered with vented plastic wrap and microcooked in less than 5 minutes per plate! Clean-up is a breeze; only one plate per person. You will find a week's worth of these recipes. Shop once and fix one each night.

Of course, you don't have to be busy to try these recipes. The important thing to remember is that microcooked meats are easily prepared and very tasty.

PORK CHOPS GRUYÈRE

4 boneless loin pork chops
   (1-inch thick)
   browning and seasoning sauce
   salt
& pepper

4 ounces Gruyère
   or Swiss cheese, grated
4-6 leaves fresh sage, chopped
2 tablespoons cream
1 1/2 tablespoons Dijon mustard
4 sprigs fresh parsley, chopped

The nutty flavor of Gruyère cheese elevates these pork chops into the gourmet category. A simple preparation yields a fabulous presentation. See index for a rice, pasta or vegetable recipe to complement this entrée.

1 Lightly brush both sides of chops with browning and seasoning sauce. Arrange chops in an 8 × 12-inch microsafe baking dish. Microcook loosely covered with waxed paper on Medium High Power (70%) 14-18 minutes, or until chops lose their pink color. Drain chops and rotate dish halfway through cooking time.

2 Sprinkle chops lightly with salt and pepper. Let stand, covered with aluminum foil, 10 minutes. (They will continue to cook during this standing time).

3 Combine the cheese, cream and mustard; spread mixture over the chops. Microcook uncovered on Medium High (70%) until cheese is melted, about 2 minutes. (Do not cook on High Power, as it will toughen the meat).

4 Sprinkle with chopped parsley and sage.

• Serves 4

The sweet potato stuffing enhances the lovely flavor of the moist roast pork in this recipe and also adds a bit of color and texture to the presentation.

ROAST PORK LOIN WITH SWEET POTATO STUFFING

1/4 cup butter or margarine
1/4 cup brown sugar
1/2 cup pecans
1/3 cup raisins
  2 tablespoons rum
1/8 teaspoon ground nutmeg

1/8 teaspoon cardamom
  1 medium sweet potato, peeled and sliced
  1 boned, rolled and tied pork loin roast (about 3 pounds)

1 If you have a clay cooking pot, soak it in water 15 minutes. Otherwise use a 9 x 12-inch microsafe baking dish for preparing this recipe.

2 In processor with steel knife, whip butter and brown sugar until smooth. Add sweet potato slices, pecans, raisins, rum, nutmeg and cardamom to the butter-sugar mixture. Process until smooth.

3 Cut 4-6 slices in pork roast 2 inches deep and 2 inches apart. Spoon potato mixture into cuts. Place remaining mixture in a microsafe bowl.

4 Place pork roast in the soaked and drained clay pot or the microsafe casserole. Microcook covered, with the clay pot lid or vented plastic wrap, on Medium Power (50%) 30 minutes. Microcook on High Power 10 minutes.

5 Check temperature with a meat thermometer. It should register 160°F. If not, remove thermometer and microcook on High Power until it reaches 160°F.

6 Let stand loosely covered with aluminum foil until roast registers 170°F on meat thermometer, about 15 minutes.

7 Microcook the sweet potato mixture on High Power 5 minutes or until steaming.

8 Slice meat and arrange on individual dinner plates with sweet potato mixture on top of meat slices.

• Serves 6-8

The even shape of a pork tenderloin or loin roast makes it ideal for microwave cooking. This flavorful, moist roast is done in no time at all. Perfect for entertaining.

FRESH HERB STUFFED PORK LOIN WITH MUSTARD SAUCE

1 (2 pound) rolled pork loin roast	kitchen string
2 tablespoons chopped fresh basil	2 tablespoons olive oil
2 tablespoons chopped fresh thyme	4 tablespoon butter
2 tablespoon chopped fresh parsley	
2 tablespoons toasted pine nuts	

1 Cut the strings on the roast and open the roast. Sprinkle one of the exposed flat sides with the chopped basil, thyme, parsley and pine nuts. Close the roast back to its original shape and re-tie with kitchen string. Brush the outside of the roast with olive oil.

2 In a heavy skillet, melt the butter. When sizzling, add the roast and quickly brown on all sides.

3 Place the roast in a microsafe rectangular casserole and microcook on High Power 10 minutes, or until a meat thermometer reaches 150°F. Wrap with aluminum foil and let stand while preparing the sauce.

Mustard Sauce

   1/2 cup chicken broth
     2 tablespoons cream
     2 tablespoons Dijon mustard
     & fresh basil leaves for garnish

4   Add the chicken broth to the remaining juices in the casserole and microcook on High Power 6 minutes, until reduced slightly. Add the cream, salt and pepper.

5   Slice the pork into 1/2-inch slices and arrange on heated dinner plates.

6   Microcook the sauce on High Power 1-2 minutes until serving temperature. Spoon over the sliced roast and garnish with fresh basil leaves.

•   Serves 4

GINGER BEEF AND VEGETABLE BUNDLES

The paper towel used for this recipe helps to steam these tasty beef and vegetable bundles. You can serve the bundles with a sprig of parsley poking out. Or you can open the bundles and spread the mixture onto the dinner plates.

4 connected paper towels
2 tablespoons soy sauce
2 teaspoon vegetable oil
1/4 teaspoon ground ginger
& fresh ground black pepper

8 ounces boneless beef sirloin steak, cut into 1/4-inch strips
2 carrots, cut into julienne strips
1 small green pepper, in 1/4-inch strips
4 tablespoons water

1 In a small mixing bowl, combine soy sauce, oil, ginger and pepper. Stir in sirloin strips. Marinate for at least 15 minutes.

2 Lay 2 connected sections of paper towel on each of 2 microsafe dinner plates. Place vegetables in center on perforations. Lift sirloin from marinade and arrange over vegetables. Fold long sides toward center, enclosing food. Fold both ends toward center overlapping on food.

3 Turn packet over, with perforated side up. Pour 2 tablespoons water evenly over each packet.

4 Microcook on High Power 5 1/2-6 minutes or until vegetables are crisp-tender. Let stand for 2 minutes. Open packet along perforations to serve.

Note: Chicken or fish could also be cooked using this method. Timing would be the same.

• Serves 2

TERIYAKI BEEF KABOBS

1/4 cup bottled teriyaki sauce
2 tablespoons orange juice
2 tablespoons honey
1 tablespoon dehydrated, chopped onion
1 tablespoon vegetable oil
1/2 teaspoon garlic powder
1/2 teaspoon ground ginger

8 (12-inch) wooden skewers
1 pound sirloin tip roast cut into 1-inch pieces
4 small onions, quartered
1 medium zucchini, cut into 16 (1-inch) chunks
8 medium sized fresh mushrooms

1 Combine teriyaki sauce, orange juice, honey, dehydrated onion, oil, garlic powder and ginger in a bowl. Place meat in a large shallow dish or a zippered plastic bag. Pour sauce mixture over meat, cover or close bag and refrigerate at least 8 hours. Drain, reserving marinade.

2 Alternately thread meat, onion, zucchini and mushrooms on 8 (12-inch) wooden skewers. Place 4 kabobs across a 9 x 12-inch microsafe baking dish with ends of skewers resting on top edge of casserole. Microcook, on High Power 6-8 minutes or to desired degree of doneness, turning and basting with marinade every 2 minutes. Repeat procedure with remaining 4 kabobs.

• Makes 8 kabobs

Prepare these yummy beef kabobs before you go to work in the morning and assemble and cook them just minutes before dinner. Hopefully, you've frozen extra wild rice or barley (see the Grain chapter). Reheat the rice, toss a nice green salad and voilà! A lovely dinner is ready in no time.

BEEF STUFFED BELL PEPPERS

Whole bell peppers make a perfect edible container for this quickly prepared dinner. Add a green salad and dinner is ready.

6 large green, red or yellow bell peppers
1 pound ground beef
2 tablespoons chopped onion
1 cup cooked rice
1 teaspoon salt
1/8 teaspoon garlic salt
1 teaspoon chopped fresh basil or 1/2 teaspoon dried basil
1 (15-ounce) can tomato sauce
3/4 cup (3 ounces) Mozzarella cheese, shredded

1 Cut thin slice from stem end of each pepper. Remove seeds and membranes, rinse peppers. Place peppers cut sides up in a microsafe pie plate or round casserole. Cover with vented plastic wrap and microcook on High Power until hot, 3-3 1/2 minutes.

2 Mix uncooked ground beef, onion, cooked rice, salt, garlic salt, basil and 1 cup of the tomato sauce. Stuff each pepper with about 1/2 cup beef-rice mixture. Pour remaining tomato sauce over peppers. Cover with vented plastic wrap and microcook on High Power 6 minutes. Rotate plate and microcook 6-8 minutes longer or until done. Sprinkle with cheese and serve.

• Serves 6

FAST FIX POT ROAST

2 cloves garlic, chopped	1 teaspoon dry mustard
1/3 cup bourbon	1/2 teaspoon beef-flavored
1 boneless beef chuck roast	instant bouillon
(about 3 1/2 pounds)	1/2 teaspoon salt
1/2 cup water	1/2 teaspoon fresh ground pepper
1/4 cup flour	3 medium potatoes, unpared, sliced
1/2 cup tomato sauce,	2 carrots, pared and sliced
combined with 1/2 cup water	2 medium onions, sliced

1 Combine the garlic and 1 tablespoon bourbon. Rub mixture into pot roast. Place roast in a 9 x 12-inch microsafe baking dish.

2 Microwave remaining bourbon in a small microsafe bowl, uncovered on High Power until hot, 20-30 seconds. Ignite and pour over pot roast.

3 Mix water and flour in a small bowl; stir in tomato sauce, dry mustard, bouillon, salt and pepper.

4 Pour the tomato-flour mixture over the roast. Cover with vented plastic wrap and microcook on High Power 15 minutes. Turn roast over and Microcook covered on Medium Power (50%) until roast is tender, about 1 hour. Add vegetables to roast during the last 30 minutes of cooking time.

• Serves 6

My grandmother was a fabulous cook, but never liked to share her recipes. As a young bride, I begged her to teach me how to fix her pot roast. Her vague instructions ended with 'and let it doodle a long time.' This recipe has the flavor of long doodling, but in about 1/4 the time.

SOUTH OF THE BORDER CASSEROLE

We all need a 'Quick Fix' ground beef casserole to serve to our families or to take to a potluck dinner. This recipe has lots of good things in it, is quickly prepared and is especially appealing to little people.

1 pound ground beef
1/2 cup chopped onion
1 (8-ounce) can tomato sauce
1/4 cup water
1 tablespoon chili powder
1 (16-ounce) can refried beans
1/4 cup taco sauce
    (mild, medium or hot,
    as you prefer)

1 1/2 cups (6 ounces)
    shredded cheddar cheese
5 taco shells, crushed
1 cup shredded lettuce
1 (6-ounce) container frozen
    avocado dip
1 small tomato, chopped
1/4 cup sliced pitted ripe olives

1   Crumble the beef in a 1 1/2-quart microsafe casserole; stir in onion. Microcook on High Power 4-5 minutes or until slightly pink, stirring 2-3 times, breaking up any lumps. Drain. Add tomato sauce, water and chili powder to meat mixture and microcook on High Power 1 minute.

2   Combine the refried beans and taco sauce in an 8 x 12-inch microsafe baking dish. Spread evenly over bottom of casserole.

3   Spread meat mixture over the beans. Microcook uncovered on High Power 5 minutes or until heated through.

4   Top with cheese. Microcook on High Power until cheese is melted, 1-2 minutes.

5   Top with crushed taco shells and lettuce. Place dollops of avocado dip over top and sprinkle with chopped tomato and sliced olives. (Individual servings reheat nicely in 1-2 minutes).

•   Serves 6-8

HONEY MUSTARD GLAZED CORNED BEEF

1 5-6 pound corned
beef brisket, rinsed well
2 cups water
3/4 cup whole-grain mustard
1/4 teaspoon cayenne pepper

3/4 cup honey
1/2 cup dark brown sugar
1 tablespoon prepared
horseradish

Your microwave makes fast work of preparing this delicious corned beef. For a new twist serve it with Creamy Whipped Potatoes and Cabbage (see index). Just think of the lovely sandwiches you can make with the leftovers!

1 Combine the brisket and water in a 4-quart microsafe casserole with a lid. Cover and microcook on High Power 12-15 minutes or until liquid reaches a rolling boil. Turn the meat over. Cover again and microcook on Medium Power (50%) 30 minutes. Turn the meat over again, cover and microcook on Medium Power (50%) 30 minutes more or until fork tender. Let the brisket stand, covered, for 10 minutes.

2 In a small microsafe bowl, combine the whole-grain mustard, cayenne pepper, honey, brown sugar and horseradish. Microcook on High Power, 2 minutes; stir until well blended.

3 To serve, transfer brisket to a microsafe serving platter, discarding the cooking juices. (If serving later, reheat in the cooking liquid on High Power 10 minutes or until boiling). Spread the brisket with 1 cup glaze. Microcook on Medium Power (50%) 10 minutes, basting twice with the juices. Let stand 15 minutes before serving.

4 Slice the corned beef very thinly across the grain. Serve warm or at room temperature. Spoon the extra glaze into a serving bowl and pass with the corned beef.

• Serves 8-10

Spaghetti squash is a wonderful vegetable. Low in calories and high in flavor, it tastes great hot or cold and can be tossed with any pasta sauce. Try this combination of flavors for an unusual simple dinner.

SPAGHETTI SQUASH WITH HAM AND PEPPERS

1 spaghetti squash (about 2 pounds)	1 medium zucchini
3 cups cubed, cooked ham or turkey ham	2 tablespoons Dijon mustard
1/2 medium red bell pepper	2 ounces light cream cheese
	3 tablespoons sunflower seeds

1 Pierce spaghetti squash in several places. Place on a microsafe plate or paper towel, and microcook on High Power 10 minutes (5 minutes per pound). Let stand ten minutes to cool.

2 Cut open the squash lengthwise, remove seeds and with a fork, comb the squash flesh. Place the resulting strands in a bowl and cover with plastic wrap.

3 Cut red pepper into thin strips and coarsely chop unpeeled zucchini. Combine the pepper strips and zucchini with the ham cubes in a microsafe bowl. Microcook covered with plastic wrap, on Medium-High Power (70%) 4 minutes.

4 Add mustard and cream cheese to vegetable-ham mixture. Re-cover with plastic wrap and microcook on Medium High (70%) 1 minute. Stir the mixture until completely blended. Re-cover the dish with plastic wrap and microcook on Medium-High Power (70%) 3 minutes. Spoon the sauce over the spaghetti squash and sprinkle with the sunflower seeds.

• Serves 4

SAUSAGE POTATO BRUNCH DISH

1 pound sausage,
    spicy or regular
1 (32-ounce) bag frozen
    hash brown potatoes
12 green onions, minced
2 cups sour cream

1 1/2 cups grated
        Cheddar cheese
2 teaspoons Worcestershire sauce
1 teaspoon salt
& freshly ground black pepper

1   Place the sausage in a microsafe 3-quart rectangular casserole.
    Microcook on High Power 4-5 minutes, stirring every 2 minutes.
    Drain and reserve sausage.

2   Place the frozen hash brown potatoes in the casserole and
    microcook covered on High Power 5 minutes, stirring and breaking
    up once. They should be slightly thawed.

3   Add the onions, sour cream, cheese, Worcestershire sauce, salt,
    and fresh ground pepper to the potatoes. Mix well.

4   Microcook, covered with vented plastic wrap, on High Power
    10-12 minutes, stirring every 5 minutes or until potatoes are
    tender.

5   Top with sausage, microcook on High Power 2-3 minutes. Let
    stand covered 5 minutes before serving.

•   Serves 8-10

Only one dish to wash when you prepare this recipe! Every part of this tasty brunch dish is prepared in one microsafe casserole. It's a great recipe for boat, cabin and RV owners.

Here's a healthy recipe for meat, potatoes and a vegetable that will satisfy hungry tummies. If you like the flavors and speedy preparation, vary it with different cooked meats, fresh broccoli florets, or zucchini chunks.

DINNER IN A POTATO

2 tablespoons cornstarch	8 ounces ham,
1 3/4 cups milk	cut into 1/2-inch chunks
1 tablespoon Dijon mustard	1 (10-ounce) package frozen
1/4 teaspoon pepper	cut asparagus, thawed and drained
1/2 cup grated Gruyère cheese	3 medium baking potatoes

1   Combine cornstarch and milk in a 2-quart microsafe bowl. Microcook on High Power, stirring every minute until thickened. 4-6 minutes. Stir in mustard, pepper and grated cheese.

2   Continue to stir until cheese is melted. Add ham and asparagus and set aside.

3   Arrange potatoes about 2 inches apart in a circle in the microwave. Microcook on High Power until tender, 10-15 minutes. Let stand 5 minutes.

4   While potatoes are resting, return the ham-asparagus sauce to the microwave and microcook on High Power 4-6 minutes or until heated through.

5   To serve, cut potatoes into halves, lengthwise. Make 1/2-inch deep cuts lengthwise and crosswise at 1/2-inch intervals in cut sides of potatoes. Push ends to open potato. Serve sauce over the top.

•   Serves 6

EGGS

Breakfast Enchiladas
Smoked Salmon Roulade
Chiles Relleno
Huevos Rancheros
Denver Omelet
Scrambled Eggs with Blue Cheese
Mushroom Avocado Scrambled Eggs
Italian Sausage Frittata
Italian Sausage Quiche
Turkey Sausage Breakfast Dish

SPEED IS OF THE ESSENCE when it comes to cooking first thing in the morning!

Microcooking Irish Oatmeal with Raisins (Grains chapter) or breakfast breads (Bread chapter) make breakfasts a breeze. Quite often you want to serve eggs. Cooking eggs in the microwave is so simple and successful that I have devoted a whole chapter to egg recipes.

Whether scrambled, poached or used in a quiche or a roulade, eggs are easy to prepare. In this chapter you'll find a number of egg dishes suitable for entertaining at breakfast or brunch. The most elegant recipe is a Smoked Salmon Roulade. It may sound tricky, but the microwave helps you every step of the way. The Roulade could also be served as a first course or as an appetizer.

To poach or soft boil an egg in the microwave, refer to the cookbook that came with your microwave. You must pierce the yolk before cooking because the yolk has a higher concentration of fat. Microwaves are attracted to water, sugar and fat so they will cook the yolk faster than the white. Piercing the yolk breaks the membrane and releases any pressure that might build up while cooking.

Hopefully, breakfast preparation just got easier. Enjoy using your microwave to produce these marvelous egg dishes.

BREAKFAST ENCHILADAS

    4 eggs
  1/3 cup cottage cheese
       salt
    4 (7-inch) snack size flour tortillas
    1 (7-ounce) can green chile salsa
    1 cup grated Cheddar cheese
       avocado slices, garnish
    & sliced green onion, garnish

1 Combine eggs, cottage cheese and salt in a microsafe bowl.
       Microcook on High Power 3-4 minutes, stirring once during
       cooking. Eggs should be slightly cooked but soft.

2 Pour 1/2 the green chile salsa in the bottom of a microsafe
       8 x 12-inch baking dish.

3 Place the tortillas on a flat surface. Divide the cooked eggs evenly
       down the center of each tortilla. Roll up and place seam side
       down in the salsa. Pour remaining salsa over top and sprinkle
       grated cheese over each rolled tortilla. Recipe can be prepared to
       this point and microcooked just before serving.

4 Microcook on High Power 2-3 minutes or until cheese is melted
       and enchiladas are heated through.

5 Garnish with avocado slices and sliced green onions.

   •   Serves 4

This is an elegant, unusual egg dish to serve at a brunch or buffet. These pinwheel slices look lovely on a pretty serving plate. If you wish, serve the roulade as an individual appetizer or first course.

SMOKED SALMON ROULADE

6 eggs
salt
fresh ground black pepper
3 ounces thinly sliced smoked salmon
1 (4-ounce) package cream cheese
1/2 cup chopped chives
& chives for garnish

1 Line a 3-quart rectangular microsafe casserole with waxed paper. Set aside.

2 Separate 4 eggs. In a small bowl, with fork or whisk, lightly beat egg yolks and 2 remaining whole eggs. Season with salt and pepper.

3 Using electric mixer at high speed, beat the 4 egg whites until stiff peaks form. Gently fold egg-yolk mixture into egg whites, just until blended.

4 Pour soufflé mixture into waxed-paper lined microsafe dish. With spatula, smooth top. Elevate dish on rack or inverted bowl. Microcook on High Power 3-4 minutes, until knife inserted in center comes out clean. This is the roulade.

5 Invert roulade onto a clean cloth towel covered with waxed paper. Peel paper off top of roulade. Starting at a long end, roll roulade with waxed paper, jelly-roll fashion. Let stand seam side down, 5 minutes.

6 Place cream cheese in a microsafe bowl and soften in microwave by microcooking on High Power 1 minute or until smooth when stirred.

7 Carefully unroll roulade. Arrange smoked salmon to within 2 inches of edges. Spread cream cheese over salmon; sprinkle with chopped chives.

8 Starting from same long end, roll up roulade without waxed paper.

9 To serve: Lift roulade with long spatula onto serving platter. Refrigerate 15 minutes. Cut into slices and garnish with chives.

• Makes 12-14 (1-inch) slices

For a nice accompaniment to a Mexican dinner, whip this up and wait for the compliments.

CHILES RELLENO

5 eggs
2 cups shredded Monterey Jack cheese
1 cup cottage cheese, well drained
1/4 cup flour
1 (4-ounce) can mild or hot chopped green chiles
1/2 teaspoon baking powder
1/2 teaspoon cornstarch

1 Beat eggs until frothy. Add the cheeses, flour, chiles, baking powder and cornstarch. Stir until well blended.

2 Pour into a microsafe pie plate or quiche dish. Microcook on Medium Power (50%) until set, about 12-13 minutes. Rotate dish if eggs appear to be cooking unevenly.

• Serves 4

HUEVOS RANCHEROS

2 eggs
2 tablespoons milk
3 tablespoons shredded
   Monterey jack cheese
2 teaspoons chopped
   green chiles, fresh or canned

salt
fresh ground pepper
1 (6-inch) corn tortilla
2 tablespoons refried beans
2 tablespoons taco sauce or salsa

Your microwave is a wonderful appliance to use for this traditional breakfast favorite. It will warm the tortilla and cook the eggs to perfection in just minutes.

1   In a small bowl whisk eggs, milk, cheese and chiles. Add salt and pepper to taste. Microcook on High Power 1 minute. Stir, drawing firmer egg from edge toward center. Cook 30 to 60 seconds longer, stirring once more, until eggs are barely set. They will continue to cook while standing.

2   Place tortilla between 2 sheets of paper towel and microcook on High Power 1 minute to soften. Transfer to dinner plate. Spread beans over tortilla; microcook on High Power 30 seconds to heat.

3   Spread eggs over tortilla and drizzle sauce over top.

Note: Multiple servings can be prepared quite easily. For four, use 8 eggs and microcook on High Power 3 minutes, stir and cook in 30 second intervals until just barely set.

• Makes 1 generous serving

DENVER OMELET

Once you prepare this traditional omelet in the microwave, you will never do it any other way. Soon you will be experimenting with other meat, seafood or vegetable omelets.

2 tablespoons butter
3 tablespoons diced ham
2 tablespoons diced green bell pepper
2 tablespoons chopped onion
4 eggs

1/4 cup milk
salt
pepper
1/4 cup shredded
    Cheddar cheese

1 In a microsafe pie plate, microcook butter on High Power 1 minute, or until melted. Stir in ham, green pepper and onion. Cook on High Power 2 minutes, stirring once.

2 In a small bowl, beat eggs with milk until blended. Season with salt and pepper to taste. Pour over ham and vegetables. Microcook on High Power 3-5 minutes, gently stirring uncooked eggs from center toward edge several times, until eggs are just set but still moist; do not overcook.

3 Sprinkle cheese over top and microcook on High Power 1 minute, just until cheese melts. Serve at once.

• Serves 2

SCRAMBLED EGGS WITH BLUE CHEESE

1/2 cup chopped green onions (green part too)
  2 tablespoons butter or margarine
  8 eggs, slightly beaten
1/2 cup milk
  2 tablespoons crumbled blue cheese
1/2 teaspoon salt
1/8 teaspoon pepper

1 Place onion and butter in a 2-quart microsafe casserole. Microcook on High Power 3-4 minutes, until onion is tender.

2 Beat eggs; add milk, cheese, salt and pepper and stir briefly.

3 Pour into casserole. Microcook on High Power 6-8 minutes, stirring every 2 minutes, until eggs are set but still moist. (Eggs will continue to cook while standing).

• Serves 4-6

The milk in this recipe helps to create fluffy and tasty scrambled eggs. The blue cheese lends a unique flavor. You'll never scramble eggs in a fry pan again once you've discovered how easy they are to prepare in your microwave.

These tasty scrambled eggs are easy to prepare. If you use a decorative microsafe bowl, they can go from oven to table.

MUSHROOM AVOCADO SCRAMBLED EGGS

```
     6  eggs
   1/2  cup sour cream or nonfat yogurt
   1/2  cup grated Cheddar cheese
     4  fresh mushrooms, sliced
   1/2  teaspoon bottled dried Herbs of Provence
        or dried oregano-rosemary
   1/2  avocado, sliced and cut into small pieces
     2  green onions, chopped
     2  tablespoons butter
        salt
     &  pepper to taste
```

1   Beat eggs with sour cream; add the cheese, mushrooms, herbs, avocado and green onion.

2   Place butter in a large microsafe pie plate or decorative serving dish. Microcook on High Power 1 minute. Tilt dish to coat bottom with butter.

3   Pour mixture into plate, sprinkle with salt and pepper. Microcook on High Power 6-7 minutes, stirring every minute. Remove from oven while still slightly soft, as eggs will continue to cook.

•   Serves 3-4

ITALIAN SAUSAGE FRITTATA

This is a well seasoned brunch dish you will enjoy serving to family and friends. You can prepare and serve it in the same dish.

  8 ounces Italian style pork
    or turkey sausage removed from casings and crumbled
1/2 red bell pepper, seeded and cut into 1/4-inch strips
1/2 green bell pepper, seeded and cut into 1/4-inch strips
  1 small red onion, quartered and cut into strips
  1 tablespoon olive oil
  4 large eggs
1/4 cup grated, fresh Parmesan cheese

1 Place the sausage meat in a microsafe pie plate. Microcook on High Power 4 minutes, stirring twice. Drain off fat. Set cooked sausage aside.

2 Combine the red and green peppers, onion and olive oil in the pie plate; microcook on High Power 5 minutes, stirring once. Stir in the reserved sausage; microcook another minute.

3 Whisk the eggs in a small bowl; stir into the hot sausage mixture. Microcook on High Power, 3 minutes, stirring twice or until the eggs are almost set.

4 Sprinkle cheese on top and cover frittata with plastic wrap. Microcook 1 minute. Let stand covered 1 minute before serving.

• Serves 4

ITALIAN SAUSAGE QUICHE

This is a nice quiche recipe for a festive brunch. It is quickly cooked in your microwave, using two unusual techniques. Whether you prepare this recipe or not, read the instructions to learn these two tricks to use in preparing other recipes.

3/4 pound sweet Italian bulk sausage
1/2 cup chopped onion
2 tablespoons flour
1 (13-ounce) can evaporated milk
4 eggs
2 cups grated sharp Cheddar cheese
1 baked 9-inch pie shell (using microsafe pie plate)
2 teaspoons fresh parsley, minced

1   In a microsafe bowl, microcook sausage and onion on High Power 4 minutes, or until crumbly. Be sure to stir while cooking.

Trick 1: Use a microsafe colander atop a shallow microsafe bowl to cook the sausage. You won't have to stir the mixture and you will avoid hard lumps, as the fat will drain off.

2   Drain fat and stir flour into sausage mixture. Microcook on High Power 1 minute.

3   Place milk in a microsafe bowl or measuring cup and microcook on High Power 2 1/2 minutes.

4   Beat eggs in a separate bowl. While beating eggs, slowly add hot milk and continue beating.

5   Add cheese to the sausage mixture and toss lightly. Spoon into baked pie shell. Pour egg-milk mixture over top. Sprinkle with parsley.

Trick 2: To insure a 'cooked' quiche center, place 2 tablespoons grated cheddar in the center of the quiche.

6 Microcook on Medium High Power (70%) until center is barely set, about 12-15 minutes. Let stand 5-10 minutes before cutting into wedges.

• Serves 6

This super simple sausage and egg dish makes a wonderful brunch entrée.

TURKEY SAUSAGE BREAKFAST DISH

1/2 pound ground turkey sausage (or pork sausage)
  3 eggs
  1 cup milk
  1 cup grated Cheddar cheese
  1 cup grated Swiss cheese
1/2 cup canned french fried onion rings
  1 green onion, minced

1   Crumble the sausage in a microsafe quiche dish or pie plate. Microcook on High Power 2 1/2 minutes, breaking up the sausage with a fork after 1 minute. Drain well.

2   Beat together the eggs and milk. Add the cheeses and french fried onion rings. Pour into the quiche dish containing the sausage. Microcook on High Power 4 minutes. Stir the cooked egg mixture into the center, allowing the uncooked mixture to come to the edge. Sprinkle with green onion. Microcook on High Power 3-4 minutes more, or until set in the center. Let stand 5 minutes.

•   Serves 4-6

SAUCES AND SPREADS

Versatile Vegetable Sauce

Lemon Curd

Strawberry Jam

Creamy Lemon Pasta Sauce with Vegetables

Caper Sauce

Herbed Spinach Tomato Sauce

Honey Mustard Pecan Sauce

Herb Butter

Horseradish Cream

Easy Mustard Sauce

Sweet and Sour Apricot Sauce

Basic Béchamel Sauce and Six Variations

Apricot-Soy Sauce

THE MICROWAVE DOES MARVELOUS magical things to sauces.

Whether it be a healthy versatile sauce for vegetables, pasta, meats or dessert; you will simply be amazed at the finished product. Try Strawberry Jam or Lemon Curd for your scones or toast, Horseradish Whip to enhance a prime rib dinner and Versatile Vegetable Sauce to create a fabulous dish for the diet conscious. This sauce will make any warm or chilled vegetable taste divine.

No more lumpy white sauces. The microwave actually prevents lumping because cooking takes place from all sides at once. Consequently there is no need to worry about scorching on the bottom as in conventional cook top cooking. Only a few quick stirs is all you need to create perfect sauces in the microwave.

Sauces can be made in the same bowl or utensil you will serve from – another nice feature of the microwave! If the sauce contains milk it is advisable to use a container or utensil double the size of the amount of milk to be used, since it could boil over.

In just a few microwave minutes, you can have wonderful tasty entrées. To add a little more flavor or taste to microcooked chicken or fish, try one of these sauces or one of your own creation. It's truly marvelous healthy dining!

VERSATILE VEGETABLE SAUCE

1 cup light or regular mayonnaise
1 tablespoon dry sherry
3 tablespoons seafood cocktail sauce
1 tablespoon sweet pickle relish

1 In a microsafe bowl, combine mayonnaise, sherry, cocktail sauce and pickle relish to form a salmon colored sauce.

2 To serve warm, microcook on Medium Power (50%) 2-3 minutes. The sauce may also be served cold.

Note: This versatile sauce can be served over hot or cold cauliflower or broccoli, or can be used as a dipping sauce for artichokes. This sauce keeps well in the refrigerator for several weeks.

• Makes 1 1/4 cups

Make up a batch of this wonderful sauce and keep it in your refrigerator. You'll find it is a lifesaver when you want a quick lunch or snack as well as making ordinary cold or hot vegetables very special.

This popular English spread is very simple to prepare in the microwave. Spread it on English muffins or croissants, use as a filling in cakes or tarts, or just top fresh fruit or berries. Small jars make wonderful hostess gifts; share the recipe as well.

LEMON CURD

1/4 pound unsalted butter
1/2 cup sugar
4 tablespoons fresh lemon juice
chopped zest of 1 lemon (grated lemon skin)
3 eggs

1 Place butter, sugar, juice and zest in a microsafe bowl. Cover with vented plastic wrap. Microcook on High Power 4 minutes.

2 Remove from oven, uncover and stir well.

3 Wisk 1/4 cup lemon mixture into the eggs to warm them; whisk constantly. Pour egg mixture back into remaining lemon mixture. Stir to combine.

4 Microcook, uncovered on High Power 2 minutes. Stir; cook for 2 minutes longer. Cool before serving. Refrigerate. Keeps several weeks.

• Makes 1 cup

STRAWBERRY JAM

     2 cups fresh strawberries
       (or fresh raspberries)
       hulled and quartered
     1 tablespoon powdered jam and jelly pectin
1 1/4 cups sugar

1 In a 2-quart microsafe container, combine the strawberries and pectin. Microcook on High Power 3 1/2 minutes or until mixture comes to a full boil.

2 Add sugar, stir well. Microcook on High Power until full rolling boil. Microcook 8-9 minutes, stirring twice during cooking.

3 Skim; let cool slightly. Stir again and pour into hot sterilized containers. Seal or store in the refrigerator in a covered container.

• Makes 1 1/2 cups

When fresh berries are plentiful, why not make up a few batches of jam? Once you make jam in the microwave you will never again do it the 'old fashioned way.'

Here's a wonderful meatless sauce for pasta. The ricotta cheese and lemon enhance the squash flavors. Makes a pretty presentation and tastes divine.

CREAMY LEMON PASTA SAUCE WITH VEGETABLES

1 cup cream
2 shallots, minced
1 clove garlic, chopped
2 teaspoons lemon zest
  (grated yellow lemon skin)
1 cup ricotta cheese
1 small zucchini,
  coarsely grated (4 ounces)

1 small yellow squash,
  coarsely grated (4 ounces)
1/2 teaspoon salt
1/2 teaspoon freshly ground pepper
2 tablespoons minced fresh parsley
1 tablespoon fresh lemon juice
1 pound pasta

1 Combine the cream, shallots, garlic and lemon zest in a microsafe casserole. Microcook on High Power 5 minutes. Let stand 5 minutes.

2 Purée the ricotta cheese in a food processor 1-2 minutes or until smooth. Set aside at room temperature.

3 Add the ricotta, zucchini, yellow squash, salt and pepper to the garlic-cream mixture. Microcook on High Power 4 minutes. Stir in the parsley and lemon juice. Taste and adjust seasonings.

4 Cook and drain pasta according to package directions. Immediately toss with warm sauce and serve.

• Makes 3 cups

CAPER SAUCE

1/4 cup nonfat yogurt or sour cream
1 tablespoon capers, rinsed and drained
1 teaspoon Dijon mustard
2 teaspoons chopped parsley
1/8 teaspoon paprika
1/8 teaspoon pepper

1 Combine the yogurt, capers, mustard, parsley, paprika and pepper in a 1-cup microsafe measure or bowl. Microcook on High Power 45 seconds or until warmed.

2 Spoon over poached salmon or poultry.

• Makes 1/4 cup

For health conscious cooks, this low fat sauce will become a favorite. It will enhance the flavors of any microoked chicken, fish or vegetable. The microwave will soon become your best friend. Just think, it's been sitting there all this time, just reheating things! Not anymore!

Chicken never tasted so good. Keep any leftover sauce in the refrigerator; then later in the week you can toss it with fresh cooked fettucine.

HERBED SPINACH TOMATO SAUCE

4 cups (packed) fresh
spinach leaves
1 medium onion, sliced
1 clove garlic, minced
1 cup canned crushed tomatoes
1 tablespoon minced
fresh basil leaves,
1/4 teaspoon fennel seeds
1/8 teaspoon dried thyme

1/8 teaspoon dried oregano
Pinch orange zest
(finely grated orange skin)
2 tablespoons chopped
Niçoise olives
1 tablespoon drained capers
crushed red pepper flakes
to taste
& goat cheese (optional)

1 Place the spinach in a microsafe casserole, cover with plastic wrap. Microcook on High Power 1-2 minutes, stirring once. Let cool, squeeze dry and finely chop.

2 Combine onion and garlic in microsafe bowl, cover and microcook on High Power 3 minutes.

3 Add the tomatoes, basil, fennel seeds, thyme, oregano, orange zest and reserved chopped spinach to the onion mixture. Microcook on High Power 2 minutes.

4 Stir in olives, capers and red pepper flakes.

5 Serve over microcooked chicken breasts, pasta or fish filets. Before serving, you might crumble goat cheese on top.

• Makes 1 1/2 cups

HONEY MUSTARD PECAN SAUCE

1 tablespoon butter
2 tablespoons finely chopped onion
1 tablespoon flour
1 cup chicken broth
2 tablespoons Dijon mustard
1 tablespoon honey
1/3 cup coarsely chopped pecans

1 In a 1-quart microsafe bowl, combine the butter and onion. Microcook on High Power 1-2 minutes, or until the onion is tender.

2 Stir in the flour until dissolved. Add chicken broth, mustard, honey and pecans. Microcook on High Power 3-4 minutes, or until thickened. Stir once during cooking.

• Makes 1 cup

Tired of eating plain chicken and fish? Prepare this zippy sauce to liven things up; it might be nice on fresh cooked broccoli as well.

Here is a lightly flavored sauce, perfect for fresh cooked fish and vegetables.

HERB BUTTER

1/4 cup chopped onions
1/4 cup butter or margarine
1 tablespoon lemon juice
1 1/2 teaspoon dried basil, crushed
& freshly ground pepper

1 Combine onions and butter in a microsafe container. Cover loosely with waxed paper.

2 Microcook on High Power 1 minute. Add the lemon juice, basil and pepper. Microcook on High Power 30 seconds.

3 Serve over warm microcooked fish filets, broccoli, cauliflower or carrots.

• Makes 1/3 cup

HORSERADISH CREAM

2 egg yolks, beaten
2 tablespoons prepared horseradish
1 tablespoon water
1 tablespoon butter
1/2 teaspoon sugar
   dash salt
1/2 cup whipping cream
1 (14-ounce) can artichoke bottoms, drained

1 In a microsafe bowl, combine egg yolks, horseradish, water, butter, sugar and salt. Microcook on Medium Power (50%) 1 minute, stir and continue to microcook on High Power until thickened. Let cool.

2 Whip the cream. Fold into the horseradish mixture and place large spoonfuls on each artichoke bottom.

• Serves 6-8

For a classy accompaniment to roast beef, ham or lamb make this lovely recipe. Using the artichoke bottoms to hold the cream really adds an elegant touch to a special dinner.

You will find many uses for this versatile sauce. Just remember to microcook it on Medium Power to avoid separation.

EASY MUSTARD SAUCE

1/4 cup sour cream or nonfat yogurt
1 teaspoon chopped green onions
2 teaspoons Dijon mustard
1/4 teaspoon prepared horseradish
(or 1/4 teaspoon lemon-pepper)

1 Combine sour cream, chopped green onion, mustard and horseradish in a microsafe bowl.

2 Cover with vented plastic wrap and microcook on Medium Power (50%) 2-3 minutes or until heated through.

Note: Serve over warm, microcooked chicken breast filets, fish filets or bright green microcooked broccoli or asparagus.

● Makes 1/4 cup

SWEET AND SOUR APRICOT SAUCE

1/4 cup apricot preserves
1 tablespoon orange juice
1 tablespoon distilled vinegar
1 teaspoon soy sauce
1/2 teaspoon Dijon mustard

1   Combine apricot preserves, orange juice, vinegar, soy sauce and mustard in a microsafe container.

2   Microcook on Medium Power (50%) 1 minute or until heated through.

Note: Spoon over warm microcooked chicken, fish or pork tenderloin slices. It is also a nice addition to microcooked carrots.

•   Makes 1/4 cup

This wonderful sauce makes ordinary tasting meats and vegetables taste superb. It is amazing what a few ingredients and one minute in the microwave can do.

If you haven't discovered how simple it is to make sauces in your microwave, get out a microsafe bowl and try one of these right now. Then find a vegetable, chicken or fish, microcook it and dinner is ready. You'll just be amazed at how quick and easy this is.

BASIC BÉCHAMEL SAUCE AND SIX VARIATIONS

2 tablespoons butter
2 tablespoons flour
1 cup milk
  dash hot red pepper sauce
  salt to taste
  fresh ground pepper to taste
& grating of fresh nutmeg, optional

1 Place butter in a microsafe bowl. Microcook on High Power 1 minute or until melted.

2 Whisk in the flour and salt until smooth and microcook on High Power 30 seconds. Gradually pour in the milk, whisking until smooth.

3 Microcook on High Power 4 minutes, whisking once. Stir until smooth and whisk in the hot red pepper sauce, nutmeg and black pepper.

• Makes 1 1/4 cups

LEMON HERB SAUCE Make Basic Béchamel sauce omitting the nutmeg. Add 3 strips lemon zest (yellow skin) to the milk. When the sauce is cooked, stir in 2 teaspoons minced fresh parsley and 1/2 teaspoon fresh lemon juice. Remove lemon strips. Serve with vegetables or fish.

CHEESE SAUCE Make Basic Béchamel sauce omitting the nutmeg. Whisk in 1 cup (4 ounces) grated Cheddar cheese and microcook on High Power 1-2 minutes or until melted. Stir to combine. Marvelous for macaroni and cheese or as a sauce for vegetables, especially cauliflower or broccoli.

MUSTARD SAUCE Prepare Basic Béchamel sauce omitting the nutmeg. Whisk in 4 teaspoons Dijon mustard and 2 teaspoons grainy mustard. Microcook on High Power 1-2 minutes. Serve with fish or pork chops.

HORSERADISH SAUCE Prepare Basic Béchamel sauce omitting nutmeg. Whisk in 2 tablespoons prepared horseradish and one teaspoon Dijon mustard. Microcook on High Power 1-2 minutes. Stir in 1 tablespoon fresh-snipped chives. This is a great sauce for roast beef or corned beef.

MORNAY SAUCE Prepare Basic Béchamel sauce omitting nutmeg. Add 1/4 cup freshly grated Parmesan cheese. Microcook on High Power 2-3 minutes. Whisk until smooth. Serve over vegetables, eggs or fish.

VELOUTE Prepare Basic Béchamel sauce using 1/2 cup cream and 1/2 cup chicken broth instead of the milk. A rich base for soup (just add puréed vegetables and more chicken broth).

- Makes 1 cup

This light, fruity sauce is wonderful on pork tenderloin slices. Fancy fare for company!

APRICOT-SOY SAUCE

1/2 cup apricot preserves
2 green onions, thinly sliced
2 tablespoons soy sauce
1 teaspooon cider vinegar
1 teaspoon dry mustard
1/4 teaspoon ground ginger

1 In a microsafe bowl combine the preserves, green onions, soy sauce, vinegar, mustard and ginger.

2 Microcook on High Power 1-2 minutes or until bubbling. Stir and pour over microcooked pork, chicken or fish.

• Makes 2/3 cup

DESSERTS

Old Fashioned Custard
Crème Caramel
Crème Brûlée
Pecan Pie Squares
Frosted Orange Squares
Cheesecake Bars
Raspberry Crumble Bars
Chilled Peach Soup
Rum Walnut Torte
Cinnamon Walnut Fresh Fruit Bake

FAT FREE DESSERT RECIPES are almost impossible to find. However, I have included 2 delightful fruit recipes: Cinnamon Walnut Fresh Fruit Bake and Chilled Peach Soup. At the other end of the spectrum I've included Pecan Pie Squares, Cheesecake Bars and other quickly fixed yummy desserts.

In developing the Crème Caramel and Crème Brûlée recipes in this chapter, it became apparent to me that the microwave was far more precise in reaching the desired brown caramel color than the stovetop method. Once the color is achieved and the microwave turned off, all microwave activity ceases instantly. You can actually watch through the glass door of your microwave as the sugar-water solution changes from clear to light brown. On the cook top, heat is retained in the metal pan and the sugar mixture continues to cook. It will often burn even when removed from the burner.

Remember when microcooking any foods, round baking dishes cook more evenly than square or rectangular ones. Because dessert surfaces will not brown, you must depend on touch to determine doneness. If the dough feels firm to the touch and is starting to pull away from the sides of the dish, it is cooked and needs no further cooking. Overcooking is the most frequent error in microwave cooking. Test for doneness by touching the surface, or by using the toothpick method (a toothpick inserted in the dough will come out clean). If more microcooking is needed, microcook in 30 second intervals until it is done.

OLD FASHIONED CUSTARD

1 1/4 cups milk
   2 teaspoons vanilla
   4 large eggs, beaten
1/4 cup sugar
   & freshly grated nutmeg (optional)

1 Combine milk and vanilla in a large microsafe bowl. Microcook on High Power 2 minutes, until hot but not boiling.

2 Meanwhile, in a medium bowl beat the eggs, sugar and nutmeg together until frothy.

3 Add the heated milk, pouring slowly and stirring constantly. Pour into four 6-ounce custard cups. Place the cups in the microwave with at least a one inch space between them. (If you place the custard cups on a large round plate or tray before cooking, they will be easier to rotate and remove).

4 Microcook, uncovered on Medium Power (50%) 6-8 minutes, or until firm, re-positioning the custards once or twice. Serve warm or chilled.

Note: To unmold and serve, run a small knife around the custard cup rim and invert the custard onto a serving plate.

• Serves 4

One day I got a desperate call from a friend. Her little boy was sick and he was begging for some custard. To cook it the regular way takes quite a little time. I gave her this recipe; her little boy loved it and she learned something new! Now you try it.

You MUST use tempered glass or a Pyrex bowl for this recipe to work. The tempered glass reaches a higher temperature that allows the sugar-water mixture to caramelize rather than crystallize.

CRÈME CARAMEL

Caramel
6 tablespoons sugar
2 tablespoons water

Custard
2 cups milk
3 eggs
3 egg yolks
6 tablespoons sugar
1 teaspoon vanilla

1   Combine 6 tablespoons sugar with 2 tablespoons water in a 2-quart round Pyrex or tempered glass casserole. Microcook on High Power about 4 minutes, just until mixture starts to turn brown. Watch through the window of your microwave and microcook in 30 second intervals until it is medium brown, not burned. If your microwave window is too dark to see the color changing, you must open the door to check the color.

2   Remove from microwave and carefully tilt dish to coat bottom and sides evenly.

3   Pour milk into a 4-cup microsafe bowl and microcook on High Power until scalded, about 3-4 minutes, watching closely so milk does not boil.

4   Whisk together the eggs, egg yolks, sugar and vanilla until blended. Slowly add hot milk, whisking constantly until thoroughly mixed. Pour into caramel coated casserole dish.

5 Microcook on Medium Power (50%) until custard begins to shrink from sides of dish, about 17-20 minutes. The custard will not be firm in the center when removed from the oven. It will set as it cools.

6 Refrigerate for at least 3 hours. To serve, run knife along edge of custard before inverting and unmolding on a decorative serving platter.

Note: You may also prepare this recipe in 6 individual custard cups, placing cups in a circle and microcooking them on High Power 17-20 minutes.

• Serves 6

My husband's favorite dessert is Crème Brûlée. We have tested this recipe so many times that he doesn't order it in restaurants anymore. Now you can enjoy the outcome of all our testing!

CRÈME BRÛLÉE

1 Prepare the custard recipe for Créme Caramel and microcook according to directions, using 6 individual porcelain ramekins or custard cups.

2 Chill thoroughly.

3 About an hour before you wish to serve the brûlée, combine 6 tablespoons sugar with 2 tablespoons water in a Pyrex measuring cup. Microcook on High Power about 4 minutes, until mixture just turns brown. Do not overcook. To be safe, microcook in 30 second intervals and watch through window of microwave for brown color. If your microwave window is too dark, you must open the door to check the color.

4 When proper color is reached, pour evenly over the chilled custards. DO NOT refrigerate. Caramel will harden and voilà! Créme Caramel is now Créme Brûlée. (If you refrigerate the ramekins, the caramelized layer will liquefy).

• Makes 6 ramekins

PECAN PIE SQUARES

Pecan pie lovers will love this recipe. Because of the high concentration of sugar, it is cooked on Medium Power.

Crust

1/2	cup butter or margarine
3	tablespoons sugar
1	egg
1 1/2	cups flour

1 Place butter in an 8-inch square microsafe baking dish. Microcook on High Power 1 minute. Add sugar, egg and flour; mix well.

2 Press evenly into bottom of dish. Microcook on High Power 4 minutes.

Filling

1	tablespoon flour	2	eggs
2/3	cup brown sugar	1/2	teaspoon vanilla
1/2	cup corn syrup	1	cup chopped pecans

1 In a mixing bowl, combine flour and brown sugar. Add corn syrup, eggs and vanilla; mix well. Stir in 1/2 cup of the chopped pecans. Pour over the baked crust. Sprinkle with remaining pecans.

2 Microcook on Medium Power (50%) 13-15 minutes. Don't overcook. Surface will be puffy and light brown. Let cool before cutting into squares.

• Makes 16 (2-inch) squares

Sipping a frosty glass of iced tea and nibbling on these refreshing orange bars is everybody's idea of heaven.

FROSTED ORANGE SQUARES

Orange Squares

1/2 cup brown sugar	1/2 teaspoon baking soda
1/4 cup butter	1/4 teaspoon salt
1 egg	1/4 cup orange juice
3/4 cup flour	1/4 cup sour cream
2 teaspoons orange zest (finely grated orange skin)	

1 Cream the butter and sugar in a mixing bowl. Add the egg. Then add the flour, orange zest, baking soda, salt, orange juice and sour cream. Beat at low speed with electric mixer 1 minute, or until well blended.

2 Spread in an 8-inch square microsafe baking dish. Place in microwave on top of an inverted microsafe bowl to elevate the dish. Microcook on High Power 4-5 minutes.

Frosting

2 tablespoons orange juice
2 tablespoon butter
1 teaspoon orange zest
1 1/2 to 2 cups powdered sugar
1/4 cup chopped walnuts

3 Combine juice, butter, and orange zest in a mixing bowl. Add sugar, beating just until smooth and of spreading consistency. Frost cake; sprinkle with chopped walnuts.

• Makes 16 (2-inch) squares

CHEESECAKE BARS

1/3 cup butter
1/3 cup brown sugar
1 cup flour
1/2 cup walnuts, chopped fine
1 (8-ounce) package cream cheese
  softened on High Power
  for 30 seconds

1/4 cup sugar
1 egg
1 tablespoon lemon juice
1/2 teaspoon lemon zest
  (finely grated lemon skin)
2 tablespoons sour cream
1 teaspoon vanilla

1 Place the butter in a microsafe mixing bowl and microcook on High Power 1 minute. Add the brown sugar, flour, and chopped nuts to the butter and mix well. Remove 3/4 cup of this mixture and set aside.

2 Press the remaining sugar-nut mixture into the bottom of an 8-inch square microsafe baking dish. Microcook on High Power 2 1/2 minutes. Let cool.

3 Beat together the softened cream cheese and sugar until fluffy. Beat in the egg, lemon juice, lemon zest, sour cream and vanilla.

4 Pour the cheese mixture over the cooled crust. Sprinkle evenly with the reserved uncooked sugar-nut mixture. Cook uncovered on Medium Power (50%) 6-7 minutes or until set in the center. Let stand at room temperature until cooled. Cover and refrigerate until thoroughly chilled. Cut into squares.

- Makes 16 (2-inch) squares

For a different taste treat, spread 4 tablespoons seedless raspberry jam between the crust and the cheesecake mixture.

These easy-to-make bars are delicious. For an interesting variation, spread a 21-ounce can of fruit pie filling between the two oat layers instead of the jam and top with vanilla ice cream for a fabulous dessert.

RASPBERRY CRUMBLE BARS

3/4 cup butter
   or margarine, softened
1 cup brown sugar
1 1/2 cups flour
1/2 teaspoon salt

1 teaspoon baking powder
1 1/2 cup quick cooking oats,
   uncooked
1 (10-ounce) jar
   seedless raspberry jam

1 Cream the butter and brown sugar until fluffy. Combine with the flour, salt, baking powder and oats.

2 Press half the oat mixture in the bottom of a greased 8-inch square microsafe baking dish.

3 Spread the jam evenly over the crust. Crumble the remaining oat mixture over the jam and press it down lightly. Microcook on Medium Power (50%) 7 minutes. Rotate dish and microcook on High Power 2 minutes. These bars firm up as they cool, so do not overcook.

4 Let stand or refrigerate 30 minutes before cutting into bars.

Note: A nice variation – substitute 10 ounces of apricot jam for raspberry jam.

• Makes 16 (2-inch) bars

CHILLED PEACH SOUP (Dessert)

1 1/2 pounds ripe peaches,
        pitted and cut into quarters
        or 2 (16-ounce) cans
        peaches, drained
   1 cup dry white wine
 1/2 cup water

1/4 cup sugar
  1 teaspoon minced,
       peeled fresh ginger
  2 tablespoons bourbon
1/4 cup nonfat yogurt

Garnish
        nonfat yogurt
      & mint leaves

1   In a microsafe bowl combine peaches, wine, water and sugar.
    Microcook, covered with vented plastic wrap, on High Power
    10 minutes, stirring twice.

2   In food processor with steel knife attached or in blender, process
    peach mixture until smooth; pour mixture through a strainer to
    remove skins.

3   Stir minced ginger into peach mixture. Microcook, covered with
    vented plastic wrap, on High Power 5 minutes, stirring twice. Stir in
    bourbon and yogurt. Refrigerate until chilled. Taste and adjust
    seasonings.

4   To serve, ladle chilled soup into bowls, wine glasses or seafood
    cocktail icer bowls. Garnish with additional yogurt and mint leaves.

•   Serves 4

Low fat desserts are hard to find. Here is one you are certain to enjoy. It is a perfect light ending for a fancy dinner and looks especially nice served in tall wine glasses or seafood cocktail icers.

For a spectacular
finale to a grand
dinner, fix this
elegant dessert.

RUM WALNUT TORTE

Torte

     3 egg whites, room temperature
  1/8 teaspoon cream of tartar
  1/2 teaspoon baking powder
     1 cup sugar
   12 graham crackers squares, crushed (about 1 cup)
     1 cup finely chopped walnuts

1 Whip egg whites with the cream of tartar until soft peaks form.
   Add the baking powder. Continue whipping while adding the sugar
   1 tablespoon at a time. Beat until well blended and thick, about
   2 minutes.

2 Fold the graham cracker crumbs and walnuts into the whipped egg
   whites. Spread into a lightly greased 9-inch microsafe pie plate or
   quiche dish. Microcook, uncovered, on Medium High (70%) 4 1/2
   to 5 minutes or until it puffs and sets but does not dry out. Cool
   at room temperature several hours. As it cools it will fall.

Topping

    1 cup whipping cream
    1 tablespoon powdered sugar
    1 tablespoon rum (or rum flavoring)
    1 teaspoon powdered coffee

3 An hour before serving, prepare the topping. Whip the cream until thick. Add the sugar, rum and powdered coffee.

4 Spread the topping over the torte and refrigerate at least 1 hour until ready to serve.

● Serves 6-8

Here is another fat free dessert. This presentation is spectacular and the flavors are so complementary. You might like to serve this for a brunch or dessert.

CINNAMON WALNUT FRESH FRUIT BAKE

1 medium grapefruit
1 medium navel orange
2 tablespoons apricot preserves
  cinnamon
1 tablespoon poppy seeds
1 tablespoon chopped walnuts

1 Peel and section grapefruit and orange and arrange on microsafe serving platter, alternating sections.

2 Warm jar of preserves (lid removed) in microwave by cooking on High Power 30-45 seconds. Drizzle apricot preserves over the fruit and sprinkle generously with cinnamon and poppy seeds. Cover with vented plastic wrap and microcook on High Power 3 minutes.

3 Remove wrap and sprinkle with walnuts. Serve warm or chilled. Nonfat frozen yogurt enhances the flavors. You might like to serve a small cookie alongside.

• Serves 4

JUST CHOCOLATE

Foolproof Fantastic Fudge

Warm Double Chocolate Brownie Pie with Raspberry Purée

Chocolate Decadence

Cocoa Cookies

Chocolate Chip Bar Cookies

Chocolate Macaroons

Chocolate Rum Balls

Rocky Road Bars

Chocolate Chip Pecan Brownies

Frozen Chocolate Dipped Bananas

Chocolate Dipped Ginger and Cashews

Chocolate Soufflé

DO YOU LOVE CHOCOLATE? Then find a recipe in this chapter and microcook a special treat. You will be amazed — no, *shocked* — to discover the fast, wonderful results.

A word of warning about cooking chocolate in the microwave. When a recipe calls for microcooking on High Power 1-2 minutes — DON'T microcook any longer and ALWAYS stir the chocolate. Chocolate squares and chips retain their shape even though melted.

The recipes in this chapter aren't fat free! The Chocolate Decadence recipe alone prevents this cookbook from being called a health conscious one. But there are times when we want to serve something rather decadent, and the recipes for Foolproof Fantastic Fudge, Chocolate Dipped Ginger, Chocolate Macaroons and Cocoa Cookies certainly fill the bill. Children love to make and eat Frozen Chocolate Dipped Bananas. You might even serve them to adults as an unusual finale to a warm summer evening dinner.

Find a chocolate recipe that appeals to you, make sure you have the ingredients and in the next week, microcook it.

FOOLPROOF FANTASTIC FUDGE

4 cups sugar
1 (14-ounce) can evaporated milk
1 cup butter
1 (12-ounce) package semi-sweet chocolate chips
1 (7-ounce) jar marshmallow creme
1 teaspoon vanilla
1 cup chopped walnuts

1   Combine the sugar, milk and butter in a 4-quart microsafe bowl or casserole. Microcook on High Power 4-6 minutes or until it boils.

2   Boil 5 minutes on High Power, stir often.

3   Mix in chocolate chips and marshmallow creme. Stir until smooth and well blended.

4   Add vanilla and nuts. Pour into a 9 x 12-inch rectangular pan.

5   Cool and cut into squares.

•   Makes 36-48 pieces

This fudge is decadent, but it makes a wonderful holiday gift. Take one bite and give the rest away. Include the recipe.

A local restaurant
serves this dessert
and MY is it
popular! While the
final product is
spectacular, it is
very easy to
prepare in your
microwave.
Chocoholics will
love it.

WARM DOUBLE CHOCOLATE BROWNIE PIE WITH RASPBERRY PURÉE

  3 large eggs
1/2 cup sugar
1/2 cup brown sugar
  1 teaspoon vanilla
  2 ounces unsweetened chocolate
  2 ounces semi-sweet chocolate
1/2 cup butter
2/3 cup flour
1/2 cup coarsely chopped walnuts
  1 quart vanilla bean ice cream
  1 (10-ounce) package frozen raspberries

Garnish
    fresh raspberries
    fresh mint leaves

1 With a mixer, beat the eggs, sugars and vanilla together for about 8 minutes or until light and doubled in volume.

2 Place chocolate squares and butter in a microsafe bowl. Microcook on High Power 2-3 minutes or until melted when stirred.

3 Fold the chocolate-butter mixture into the egg mixture. Fold in the flour and nuts. Pour into a 10-inch microsafe pie plate and smooth the top evenly with a spatula.

4 Place an inverted microsafe cereal bowl in the microwave oven and place the pie on top. Microcook on Medium Power (50%) 8 minutes, then on High Power 3-4 minutes or until a toothpick comes out clean. Let stand for 10-20 minutes directly on the counter. (If not serving until the following day, cover tightly with plastic wrap). To serve warm, microcook covered on Medium Power (50%) 3-4 minutes.

5 Purée frozen raspberries in processor and strain through a fine sieve to remove the seeds. You might sweeten the purée with a little sugar.

6 Ladle a pool of raspberry purée on each dessert plate. Cut pie into wedges and place on each plate. Top each wedge with a scoop of ice cream and garnish with fresh raspberries and mint leaves if desired.

- Serves 6-8

CHOCOLATE DECADENCE

This is the most decadent, high fat, fabulous dessert in the book. Chocolate lovers will love it. It is most elegant if presented with the suggested chocolate leaves or, for a colorful touch, I have served it with tiny Johnny-Jump-Up blossoms.

    1   pound semi-sweet chocolate, broken into pieces
    1   cup milk
  1/8   teaspoon salt
1 1/2   cups butter, at room temperature
    7   egg yolks

1 Butter bottom and sides of a 9-inch springform pan.

2 Place chocolate, milk and salt in a large microsafe bowl. Microcook on High Power 3 minutes. Stir and cook in 1 minute intervals until smooth.

3 Using slow speed of an electric mixer, mix and add slices of butter and egg yolks. (Do not beat on high speed).

4 Pour into the prepared springform pan. Bake in conventional oven at 350°F for 25 minutes, no longer. It will be soft and shining, and will not look done. It may even be runny in the middle. Let stand at room temperature until cool. Refrigerate until completely set. Can be prepared the day before serving.

Chocolate Leaves

   1 square semi-sweet chocolate
   12 green leaves

5 To make chocolate leaves; microcook chocolate on High Power 1 minute or until melted. With pastry or artist's brush, brush chocolate on underside of stiff green leaves (camellia or rose leaves are perfect).

6 Place chocolate coated leaves on tray in refrigerator or freezer. When hardened, carefully peel leaf from chocolate, being careful not to melt chocolate from warmth of your hands. A pattern of the veins on the leaves will be imprinted in the chocolate. Place leaves around edge of dessert and cut into wedges to serve.

- Serves 12-16

As you know, microwaves don't brown food, but here the cocoa disguises the fact that the cookies aren't browned. DON'T overcook, as they burn easily below the surface where you cannot see the damage. Remember, microwaves are attracted to 3 things: water, sugar and fat. The high concentration of sugar and fat within the cookie dough causes the inside to reach a higher temperature faster than the top or underside.

COCOA COOKIES

3/4 cup butter or margarine
3/4 cup sugar
  1 egg
1 3/4 cups flour
1/4 cup unsweetened
     cocoa powder

  1 teaspoon baking powder
1/2 teaspoon salt
  1 teaspoon vanilla
1/2 cup chopped walnuts
     granulated sugar for coating

1 Combine butter, 3/4 cup sugar and egg with an electric mixer until light and fluffy.

2 In another bowl mix together the flour, cocoa, baking powder and salt.

3 Combine the flour-cocoa mixture with the butter-egg mixture and stir together just until blended. Stir in vanilla and nuts.

4 Roll dough into 10 (1-inch) balls. Sprinkle sugar in a shallow bowl. Roll the balls in the sugar. Chill balls until ready to bake.

5 Place balls 1-2 inches apart on a large microsafe plate. Flatten tops slightly with a spoon. Microcook on High Power 2 1/2 minutes or until cookies are puffed. For crisper cookies, let cook an additional few seconds. Let cool slightly before removing from the plate. They will get firm as they cool. Transfer to rack and cool completely. Repeat with remaining dough.

• Makes 30 cookies

CHOCOLATE CHIP BAR COOKIES

1/4 cup butter or margarine
3/4 cup packed brown sugar
   1 egg
1 1/3 cups Bisquick
1/2 cup chopped walnuts
   1 (6-ounce) package chocolate chips

1   Cream the butter and brown sugar until smooth. Beat in the egg.
    Stir in the Bisquick, nuts and chocolate chips. Stir until well
    combined.

2   Spread the dough in a lightly oiled microsafe 8 x 8-inch square
    baking dish. Microcook uncovered on High Power 4 1/2-5 1/2
    minutes. Cover loosely with waxed paper to retain moisture and
    let stand at least 10 minutes before cutting into squares.

•   Makes 16-20 bars

Thanks to a Bisquick
Baking Mix and the
microwave oven,
you'll have a head
start in preparing
these wonderful bar
cookies.

With supervision, children can have fun making these wonderful morsels that everyone will enjoy eating.

CHOCOLATE MACAROONS

1 ounce unsweetened chocolate
2/3 cup (half a 14-ounce can) sweetened condensed milk
1 1/3 cup flaked coconut
1 teaspoon vanilla

1 Place chocolate in a 2-quart microsafe casserole. Microcook on High Power 1-2 minutes or just until melted. Be certain to stir once during cooking time.

2 Add sweetened condensed milk, flaked coconut and vanilla to the chocolate. Stir to combine. Microcook on High Power 6-7 minutes or until mixture loses its gloss, stirring every 2 minutes.

3 Immediately drop by spoonfuls onto waxed paper, pressing together with fingers if necessary.

4 Cool and store in airtight container.

Note: At holiday time you might use white chocolate and tint half the mixture with red food coloring and the other half with green.

• Makes 36 macaroons

CHOCOLATE RUM BALLS

1 1/2 cups chocolate chips
   1 (8-ounce) package cream cheese
1/2 teaspoon vanilla
   1 (9-ounce) package chocolate wafer cookies,
     crushed (about 3 cups)
   1 cup finely chopped pecans
   2 tablespoons rum or rum flavoring
   & powdered sugar

1 Place chocolate chips and cream cheese in a microsafe bowl. Microcook on High Power 1-2 minutes or until melted enough to combine.

2 Add vanilla, crushed cookies, chopped pecans and rum to the chocolate-cream cheese mixture. Combine and roll into 1-inch balls. Roll in powdered sugar. Refrigerate covered.

• Makes 36 balls

These are nice chocolate treats to serve at holiday time. They also make a lovely hostess gift. Most importantly, they are very easy to prepare, thanks to the microwave.

These bars are decadent and are usually gobbled up fast. The ingredients are very portable and you only use one microsafe baking dish. This makes it a great recipe for college students, cabin, boat and RV owners. This little treat can be made anywhere you go, providing you have access to a microwave.

ROCKY ROAD BARS

1 (6-ounce) package chocolate chips
1 (6-ounce) package butterscotch chips
1/2 cup butter or margarine
3/4 cup creamy peanut butter
2 cups miniature marshmallows
6 ounces salted peanuts

1 Put chips, butter and peanut butter in an 8 x 12- or 9 x 13-inch microsafe baking dish. Microcook on High Power 2-3 minutes or until melted. Stir well. Cool.

2 Add marshmallows and peanuts; stir to combine. Refrigerate. When firm, cut into squares.

• Makes 24-30 large squares

CHOCOLATE CHIP PECAN BROWNIES

You'll get a double dose of chocolate in these brownies. They are good!

2 ounces (2 squares) unsweetened baking chocolate
1/2 cup butter
2 eggs
3/4 cup sugar
1/2 cup flour
2 teaspoons vanilla
1 teaspoon baking powder
1/4 teaspoon salt
1 cup coarsely chopped pecans
1 cup chocolate chips

1 In a 1-quart microsafe bowl, microcook unsweetened chocolate and butter on High Power 1 1/2 minutes, or until butter is just melted. Stir several times while cooking. Blend well.

2 In another bowl, beat eggs. Add melted chocolate and butter, sugar, flour, vanilla, baking powder and salt. Blend well. Stir in pecans and chocolate chips. Pour batter into a microsafe pie plate, quiche dish or square baking dish.

3 Place an inverted microsafe bowl in the microwave. Place the pie plate of brownie batter on top of the bowl and microcook on High Power 5-6 minutes or until brownies begin to pull away from the sides of the container.

4 Brownies will be moist but will firm up as they cool. Let cool completely before cutting into wedges or squares. You may serve glazed with chocolate topping or with a scoop of vanilla ice cream.

• Makes 10-12 wedges or 16 squares

FROZEN CHOCOLATE DIPPED BANANAS

If you want to be well liked by your children or grandchildren just have them help you whip up a batch of these wonderful bananas-on-a-stick. You can buy them in a grocery store, but it's lots more fun to watch little people make their own. Sometimes you never see the finished product, it is gobbled up so quickly.

 4 medium bananas
 4 sturdy wooden skewers
 1 cup chopped pecans
 2 tablespoons butter
10 ounces bittersweet or semi-sweet chocolate

1 Cover a large plate with waxed paper. Peel the bananas and skewer them lengthwise with the wooden skewers. Put the bananas on the plate, cover with more waxed paper and freeze for at least 1 hour.

2 Place the chopped pecans on a microsafe dinner plate. Microcook on High Power 2-3 minutes or until lightly toasted.

3 Place the butter and chocolate in a microsafe pie plate. Microcook on High Power 2-3 minutes, stirring every 30 seconds, or just until melted.

4 Coat the frozen bananas first with the warm chocolate and then with the pecans. Return to the freezer on the waxed-paper-covered plate. Freeze until the chocolate hardens, or at least 30 minutes. Serve frozen.

• Serves 4

CHOCOLATE DIPPED
GINGER AND CASHEWS

1/4 cup crystallized ginger
1/4 cup coarsely chopped cashews
  8 ounces bittersweet or semi-sweet chocolate

The wonderful taste of candied ginger combined with chocolate and cashews makes for a most unusual 'quick and easy' candy treat.

1 Mince crystallized ginger with a sharp knife. Do not use processor.

2 Place cashews on a microsafe plate and microcook on High Power in 2 minute intervals until lightly toasted, 4-6 minutes. Stir every 2 minutes.

3 Place chocolate in a microsafe bowl. Microcook on High Power 1-2 minutes, stirring after one minute, just until melted.

4 Add the ginger and cashew pieces to the melted chocolate and mix well.

5 Drop by rounded teaspoonfuls onto a waxed paper lined baking sheet. Let stand until hardened (about 30 minutes), placing in the refrigerator if necessary. Store in a covered container in refrigerator up to 3 weeks.

• Makes 24 pieces

CHOCOLATE SOUFFLÉ

Many restaurants feature chocolate soufflés on their menus and require 20 minutes notice to prepare them! Now you can make your own chocolate soufflé in the microwave, in just 5 minutes! To make it even simpler, prepare the batter a day ahead.

    6 tablespoons butter
    4 ounces semi-sweet chocolate
3/4 cup sugar
    2 tablespoons cornstarch
    3 eggs

1   Place the butter and chocolate in a microsafe bowl. Microcook on High Power 1 1/2 to 2 minutes. Stir until smooth.

2   Combine the sugar and cornstarch in a bowl. Add chocolate mixture and stir well to combine.

3   In another bowl, beat the eggs with an electric mixer. Add the eggs to the sugar-chocolate mixture. Fold in eggs until well combined.

4   Refrigerate the soufflé batter overnight. When ready to cook the soufflé, pour batter into 4 individual porcelain ramekins. Place ramekins in a circle in the microwave. Microcook 5 minutes. Serve immediately while still warm.

Note: You might top the soufflés with a spoonful of seedless raspberry jam, powdered sugar, whipped cream or vanilla bean ice cream. Remember that soufflés collapse a bit when removed from the oven.

•   Serves 4

COOKBOOK ORDER FORM

Copies of *The Marvelous Microwave* are available at $18.95 per copy.

QUANTITY	PRICE/COPY	COST
_____ THE MARVELOUS MICROWAVE	18.95	_____

Other microwave cookbooks available from Creative Cookery.

_____ THE EVERDAY GOURMET	15.95	_____
_____ MARVELOUS MICROWAVE POPCORN	5.95	_____
Postage and Handling per book (4 or more books free postage)	2.50	_____
California residents add 8.25% State Sales Tax		

TOTAL COST $ _____

Make check or money order payable to: CREATIVE COOKERY

Mail with order form to: Creative Cookery
PO Box 437
Alamo, CA 94507-2312

Questions, or for fast delivery FAX: 510-838-6939

Mail book to:

NAME _____

ADDRESS _____

CITY/STATE/ZIP _____

Autograph to: _____

Use other side of form for additional addresses

COOKBOOK ORDER FORM

Copies of *The Marvelous Microwave* are available at $18.95 per copy.

QUANTITY	PRICE/COPY	COST
_____ THE MARVELOUS MICROWAVE	18.95	_____

Other microwave cookbooks available from Creative Cookery.

_____ THE EVERDAY GOURMET	15.95	_____
_____ MARVELOUS MICROWAVE POPCORN	5.95	_____
Postage and Handling per book (4 or more books free postage)	2.50	_____
California residents add 8.25% State Sales Tax		

TOTAL COST $ _____

Make check or money order payable to: CREATIVE COOKERY

Mail with order form to: Creative Cookery
PO Box 437
Alamo, CA 94507-2312

Questions, or for fast delivery FAX: 510-838-6939

Mail book to:

NAME _____

ADDRESS _____

CITY/STATE/ZIP _____

Autograph to: _____

Use other side of form for additional addresses

NOTES